Rural Life
in the Dun Valley

1066 – 1900

Margaret Baskerville

Looking across West Dean towards the yew trees on Dean Hill. (AB)

Rural Life in the Dun Valley

1066 – 1900

Margaret Baskerville

First published in the United Kingdom in 2010 by Margaret Baskerville, Owls' Castle, Easton Common Hill, Winterslow, Salisbury SP5 1QD

Printed and bound by Baskerville Press, Salisbury, Wiltshire

A CIP catalogue record for this book is available from the British Library

ISBN 978-0-9566392-0-2

Contents

Acknowledgements

A book of this nature is not produced by the efforts of the author alone, and I am indebted to my husband, Arthur, without whose advice, help and encouragement it could not have been written. I would also like to thank the staff of the Hampshire Record Office, Winchester, the Wiltshire and Swindon History Centre, Chippenham, and Salisbury Library Local Studies Section for their helpful assistance and patience.
Our sincere thanks to Judeth Dashwood at Baskerville Press for all her help and support during the design and presentation of this publication.

Illustrations

Colour pictures are numbered separately in Roman numerals.

My thanks are due to the following for permission to use the illustrations as indicated in the figure captions:

Arthur Baskerville (AB), the Hampshire Record Office (HRO) and the Wiltshire and Swindon History Centre (WSHC).

In addition I would like to thank the Weald and Downland Open Air Museum, Singleton, Chichester, Sussex for permission to publish figures XV, XVI, XVII, and XVIII.

Other illustrations are from the following:

T. Bewick. A General History of Quadrupeds, 1790. Figs.17, 19 & 25, title page, back cover.
G. A. Thrupp. The History of Coaches, 1877. Fig. 33.
W. Harrison Ainsworth. Ovingdean Grange, 1860. Fig. 11.
R. Colt Hoare. The History of Modern Wiltshire, 1837. Fig. 7.
Punch magazine 1841-60. Figs. 23, 26, 27, 36.

The diagrams as indicated (MB) and line drawings are by the author.

I
Setting the Scene

The River Dun, described in 19th century trade directories as 'a rivulet in a pleasant valley', is a tributary of the River Test, which runs across the southern part of Wiltshire and flows eastwards into Hampshire to join the Test at Kimbridge near Mottisfont. South of the river Dean Hill rises abruptly from the valley to a height of 150m above sea level, forming a ridge about four miles long. The northern face of the hill is a steep slope for much of its length, covered in places with a spectacular mass of naturally-grown yew trees, interspersed with deciduous trees such as whitebeam. The Ministry of Defence occupies a section of the hillside, but has not dramatically altered its appearance, apart from the radio mast on the summit which forms a familiar landmark for many miles around. Large parts of the northern side of the hill are managed by Natural England, thereby providing protection for both the trees and the flora of the grassland, which include juniper bushes and many orchids. Cowslips and primroses encourage the uncommon Duke of Burgundy butterflies to breed there. To the north of the river the land rises more gradually, and is heavily wooded along much of the valley, particularly at the western end where the 1700 acres of Bentley Wood occupy a large part of West Dean parish. This stretch of woodland belongs to a Charitable Trust which combines forestry with the development of a nature reserve, and like Dean Hill has been designated a Site of Special Scientific Interest. Eastwards from West Dean there are further patches of woodland right across to the Test Valley, so that the view to the north from Dean Hill looks down over a fairly wooded landscape.

The Dun, or Dean, Valley region lies at the junction of the chalk downland to the north and the very different countryside of the Hampshire Basin in the south, which includes the New Forest. Fifty to sixty million years ago marine sediments formed over parts of southern England covering the underlying chalk, much of which had eroded away by that time. The deposits of clay and sand, together with the remains of flints from the eroded chalk, formed the Hampshire Basin (Fig. 2), and these Tertiary sediments begin around East and West Tytherley where there are fields of light well-drained chalk soil in close proximity to areas of thick sticky clay. Dean Hill rises as a chalk ridge, the very last of the chalk before the Hampshire Basin, and there are the remains of a parallel low ridge on the north side of the

Dun Valley. This partial ridge inhibits the drainage of the heavy soils to the north into the Dun so that southward flowing streams divert round the hills to drain into the river, and there are also swallow holes where the water disappears underground before emerging again in the valley. Originally, the Salisbury Avon and its tributaries, which drain large parts of Wiltshire, flowed eastwards along the north side of Dean Hill to join with the Test and the Itchen before running down what is now Southampton Water and the Solent. The coastline at that time was out beyond the Isle of Wight. This deepened the Dun Valley to a far greater extent than the present small stream could have done, and deposited material there which had originated in the area drained by the Avon. Eventually the river in what is now the lower part of the Avon valley broke through the intervening ridge capturing the Avon, which from that time onwards began to flow along its present course due south to Christchurch, leaving the steep-sided Dun Valley with a small stream collecting water from the local area only[1,2].

Today, the River Dun collects water from Clarendon and the land around the Grimsteads, and is added to by water from the region west of the Test before it joins the main river. Water levels in the Dun would have varied through the centuries depending on the rainfall at the time, but despite changes in water extraction, the river level during the time period we are considering appears likely to have been similar to that of today. The Dun was never big enough to be a navigable river, and it was not deep enough to act as a barrier to mobility as it could be crossed quite easily at any point. It was, however, sufficiently large to provide a dependable water supply, and the lower reaches were adequate to turn a mill wheel.

The names Dun and Dean describe the physical structure of the area, and are among the most commonly used names from Anglo-Saxon times. Dun is Old English for a hill, as in the modern 'down', but was originally taken from the Celtic word *duno-* with the same meaning. It was current in the Romano-British period and was important in place-names throughout Roman Britain. Dean is from the Old English *Denu*, a valley, usually implying a long narrow valley with moderately steep sides and a gentle gradient along its length[3]. The geology and geography of any landscape play an important part in its history, affecting whether man settles there, and the subsequent land use through the ages. The Dun Valley is no exception, and the valley attracted settlers from prehistoric times onwards, making use of the river and the valley soil for agricultural crops, as well as the grazing land and woods beyond. The clay soil provided good growing

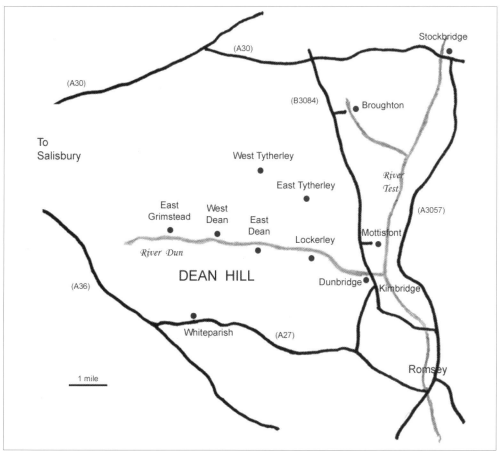

Fig. 1 *The area around the Dun Valley to show the villages, rivers and principal roads (MB)*

conditions for oak trees, a valuable and much-used timber throughout history, while the chalk grassland, both on Dean Hill and on chalk areas to the north, provided ideal grazing for flocks of sheep. The soil and subsoil material were also utilized by the local inhabitants. The chalk was used for building, plastering and as a useful fertilizer for the agricultural land, while the deposits of good-quality clay provided material for several brickworks in the area.

In order to study the history of the people who lived in and around the Dun Valley it is necessary to define the extent of the region to be investigated. For the past 1000 years people have been identified with parishes, and the parish provides a historically stable area which still exists today. There have been some well-recorded changes to parish boundaries but overall they have remained constant, and the Dun Valley has therefore been taken to include principally East Grimstead, West Dean, East Dean, Lockerley and East Tytherley parishes. East Tytherley is included because it was historically linked with Lockerley, and the combined manors of East Tytherley and Lockerley controlled a significant portion of the valley. The surrounding parishes of West Tytherley, Broughton and Mottisfont also have to be included to a limited extent, since manors there held land along the valley and are consequently part of its history. Broughton included Frenchmoor, a parish detachment on the edge of the Dun Valley, while Mottisfont Priory, and the secular estate which inherited it, held land in East Dean, as did the manor of Norman Court in West Tytherley. The churches were also partly interlinked, since East Dean and Lockerley were both chapels attached to the church of Mottisfont.

The time period, 1066 - 1900, was chosen because it allowed more detail to be included, rather than attempting to describe the history of life in the area from prehistoric times down to the 21st century. The great volume of records from the 20th century would swamp the earlier information if they were to be included here. However, the time before 1066 needs some consideration as it has a bearing on the subsequent history. The Norman Conquest was a considerable upheaval, and makes a good starting point, but the social structure of the Dun Valley had already been established during the preceding centuries.

Under Roman occupation from 55BC until the 5th century AD, the country experienced not only control by an army of occupation, but also for the first time a unified system of government. Heavy taxes were imposed on the local population, but the money raised was spent within the country and a money-based economy was established in Britain. Winchester became a Roman administrative centre and it was on the network of the new roads which were constructed for military, trade and administrative purposes. One of these roads led westwards to Old Sarum, the original site of Salisbury, where an Iron Age hillfort close to a crossing-point of the Avon and also on an important road junction, provided a suitable place for the Romans to establish a small town.

During the occupation some of the native British population prospered, and adopted the Roman way of life. In the countryside local estate owners, who had profited by providing agricultural products to the occupying army and the growing towns, built Roman-style villas, complete with bath houses and hypocaust heating systems. The valley soil of the Dun Valley supported three such villa estates in relatively close proximity to each other at East Grimstead, West Dean and Holbury, the remains of which must have been part of the local folk-lore during the centuries that followed.

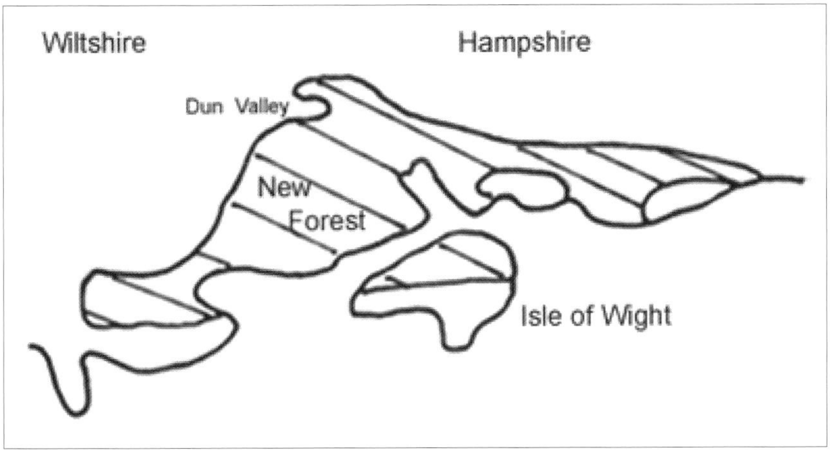

Fig. 2 *The Hampshire Basin (MB)*

The retreat of the Roman armies left Britain vulnerable to invasion by sea-going tribes from continental Europe. During the 5th century the Saxons settled in south-east England, fighting the native Britons for control of the land there, so that by *c* 450 Wessex was surrounded on its eastern side by

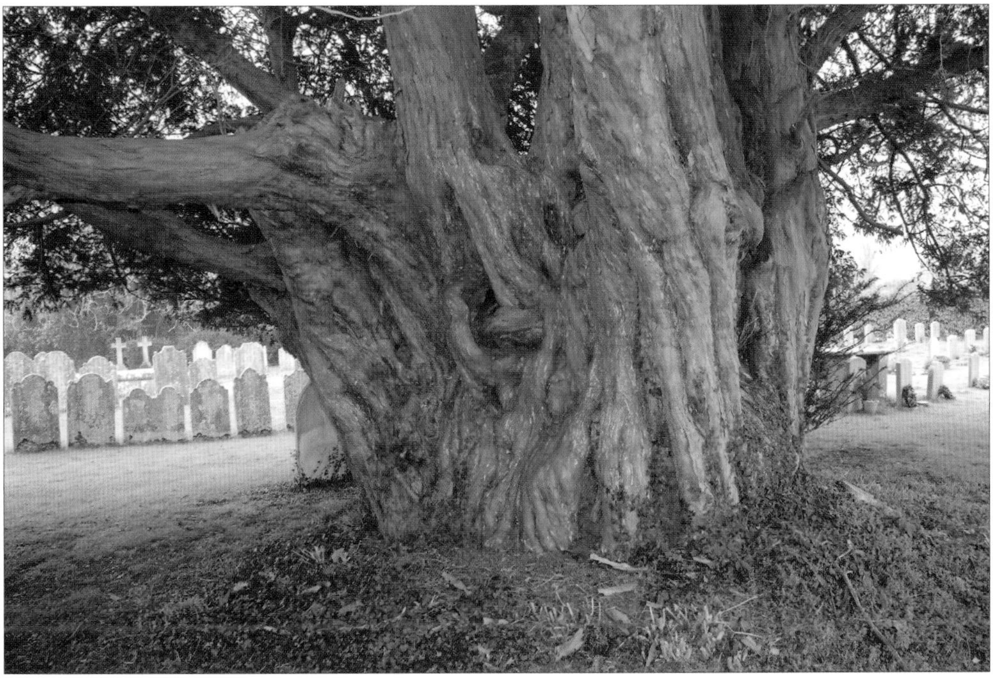

Fig. I *Ancient yew tree in Lockerley churchyard.(AB)*

Saxon settlers. Further waves of Saxon invaders penetrated the region by coming in from the sea up the river estuaries, including the Avon[4]. Other parts of England suffered similar invasion, and once again it became a land of tribal areas. Wessex had become a separate kingdom by 839, as had East Anglia and Mercia[5]. Raids by the Danes followed later, but by that time Wessex had become a stronger cohesive unit, and the Danes were defeated by King Alfred, so that while they occupied the eastern side of England, Wessex remained independent. There was therefore far less Danish influence on the language and place-names than in some parts of the country.

Winchester became the capital of what was now the local kingdom of Wessex, ruled by its own king, of whom the most famous was Alfred the Great. While maintaining an administrative centre at Winchester, the Saxon kings moved around their kingdom, staying at their royal villas as they did so. These villa estates became the nuclei for local settlements and area centres of administration. Broughton, King's Somborne and Wallop were all royal villas, and continued to be so in Norman times. The Saxon nobility, or thegns, who held land in return for services to the king, became the estate owners around the Dun Valley, and Saxon settlements developed along the river, where the Romano-British villas had once stood. The local population of the region were now Saxons, speaking Old English and culturally different from the British race which they had displaced.

Christianity had been established in Wessex in the 4th century under Roman rule, and it is likely that it continued in places during the pagan Saxon invasion. The conversion of Saxon Wessex began in 635 and Winchester became an important ecclesiastical centre. Further west the centres were Ramsbury and Sherborne, which were united in 1050 when the Episcopal seat was moved to Old Sarum. Under the Saxons minster churches were developed, where priests and monks lived communally, initially in centres such as Winchester, but subsequently many minor minster churches were built. From about 700 onwards these priests, whose role was to care for the spiritual life of the scattered population, travelled out to the villages and preached Christianity to the villagers in the open air, often at a stone cross to mark the site. This was gradually replaced by local churches, provided by the thegns on their estates, and the village church came into being[6]. Many of these early churches, particularly in areas with no local stone, were simple timber buildings. The custom of planting yew trees in churchyards dates back to Saxon times, and may have been a continuation of a previous pagan custom. The yew is a very long-lived tree species and there are a number of very ancient churchyard yews still in existence today. Two venerable old specimens stand in the churchyard at Lockerley, one of which has a girth of more than 25 ft., indicating that it has overseen the village history since the Norman Conquest, and probably for a few hundred years before that (Fig.I, p5). Estate village churches often became later parish churches and there is a close association between the extent of Anglo-Saxon estate boundaries and later ecclesiastical parish boundaries[7].

By about AD 1000 the countryside of Wessex had largely become the landscape conquered by the Normans 60 years later. The language and culture of the ruling classes changed following the Norman Conquest, but the social structure of villages remained the same. The Normans ensured that they remained in control, and built fortified castles and dwellings to prevent uprisings along vulnerable borders, but they did not displace the general Anglo-Saxon population.

Fig. II *Former site of East Tytherley manor, and the church beyond.(AB)*

Fig. III *The remains of the 'dyke' around East Tytherley medieval park.(AB)*

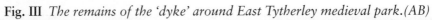

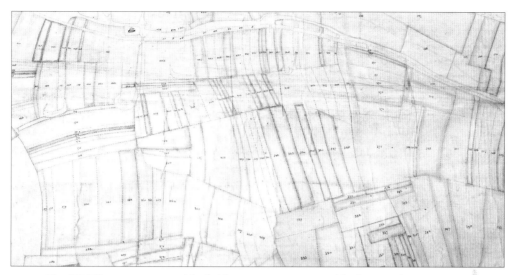

Fig. IV *The common arable fields in East Grimstead before enclosure, 1845.*
WSHC ref. 451/349 (AB)

Fig. V *The same area today. (AB)*

2
Medieval Times

When the Domesday survey was compiled in 1086, twenty years had passed since the Norman Conquest. The survey was designed so that the king could find out precisely who held all the land in the country, what it had been worth before the conquest, and what its current value was. The Saxon system of taxing the productivity of all the manors which controlled the land, except those which were directly held by the king, was thereby brought up to date and expanded.

The countryside around the Dun Valley, and life for its peasant farmers, would not have changed very dramatically under the new regime, except that the ruling class were now foreigners. The Anglo-Saxon manor, with its communal system of open-field agriculture, had been very similar to the Norman equivalent which took over the land. To be self-sufficient a manor needed water, suitable arable land to grow cereal crops, grazing land for the animals and woodland as a source of wood. Wood was required not only as building timber but also for making hurdles, tools, implements, gates and carts, and for the greatest use of all, fuel for heating and cooking. When these fundamental requirements could not be obtained locally, the manor had to look further afield, and it was not unusual for Saxon or early Norman manors to hold outlying areas of land, or to have common grazing rights beyond their own estate borders. Cattle and sheep might be driven to distant grazing land during the summer, or wood fetched from a wooded area some miles away.

The feudal system

The feudal system and land tenure were a fundamental part of rural life in medieval England. A brief description of the system as it had developed under the Norman kings and their successors, and its gradual evolution over the following centuries, is therefore necessary for an understanding of the history of the Dun Valley villages. Following the Norman Conquest all land that was not directly retained by the Crown was 'held' from the king by the Tenants-in-Chief, or major landlords, in return for either a commitment to provide a certain number of armed soldiers when required, or the performance of specified duties, such as being the king's principal huntsman, forester or standard-bearer. This land was then sub-infeudated, or sublet, in smaller parcels, the holders of which also had commitments to their overlord. Although estates were held from the king rather than owned, land and titles could be inherited down through the family, normally passing to the eldest son. However if there were no issue, or the land-holder had forfeited his estates, having committed a major offence or in some way displeased the king, the land passed back to the Crown. The manor and title were then transferred as gifts to someone else.

At a local level the lord of the manor controlled the land on the manor estate, and people living within the manor owed a range of obligations to him. The nature of their obligations varied, depending on the tenure under which they held their land. Freehold tenure, or socage, was less 'free' than it is today. A sum of money, or relief, followed by an annual rent, which was often nominal, was paid when succeeding to the property. The freeholder could then dispose of his property as he wished and could bequeath or sell it. He did not have to ask permission to depart from the manor but certain obligations were owed to the lord of the manor by freeholders, such as suit of court once or twice a year, which involved taking part in the manor court proceedings and decisions.

Reaping Corn

Unfree tenants formed a much larger group. Villeins usually held a virgate (yardland) of about 30 acres, or half virgate, of land, bordars or cottars were smallholders and they held about 6 acres. These unfree tenants held their land in return for regular work on the demesne land, which was land retained and farmed directly by the lord and not let out to tenants. In addition to working for part of each week they were required to give extra help during haymaking and harvest. The unfree tenant was tied to his land, and he could not leave the manor to work elsewhere without the lord's permission. He paid an entry payment, or 'fine', when he originally took on his land, followed by a small rent, and had to make a 'merchet' payment to the lord when his daughter married. When he died his successor had to give a 'heriot', the best beast on the holding, to the lord. The unfree tenant also owed regular appearances at the manor court, rather than occasionally like the freeholders.

Landlords let out some of their land as leasehold, originally called 'at farm', and the whole manor or the demesne was sometimes leased out. Leaseholds could be held for lives or years, commonly 99 years based on three lives. The leaseholder paid a high entry fine followed by a modest rent, which could not be increased, but this changed in later centuries to shorter leases with more realistic rents[1].

The manor tenants also had rights on the manor estate lands which were essential to their way of life. These rights included grazing for their animals on the manorial waste, or uncultivated common land, pannage for their pigs in the woodland, wood from the hedgerows and coppices and extraction rights of chalk, clay and peat. The manorial rights were held according to what was known as the 'custom of the manor', or the rights and duties of the tenants which had been in existence 'since time out of mind', and which was used as the basis for the ruling by the manor courts. The numbers and species of animals which were allowed to graze were specified, so too were the exact dates of the grazing period. Any additional or stray animals on any of the manor land were driven into the local pound, and kept in custody until their owners paid to have them released. A certain amount of wood was allowed, such as fallen wood for fuel and wood to mend fences and carts, and for home repairs. The timber trees belonged to the lord of the manor and could not be touched, although he granted limited quantities for construction and repairs to buildings and local bridges.

The farming in the Dun Valley was carried out in an open field system. Although each freeholder or unfree tenant held a certain acreage of land, it was not as a discrete holding with enclosed fields. The tenants' arable land, and often much of the demesne arable as well, was in fragmented lots spread across three or four big open fields. The pasture land was held in common, so that everyone's animals grazed together in a common herd or flock. In medieval times, before the advent of modern fertilizers, the nutrition in the soil was exhausted after it had grown crops for two successive years, and it was then left fallow during the third year to recover. The fallow time was not completely wasted as some plants grew up on it naturally and it was then used for grazing land. Each open field was divided up into blocks of furlongs, and by common agreement each block was sown with a certain crop. The tenants had strips of land in different blocks and in the fallow, so that everyone had a reasonably fair distribution (Fig.IV, p9). The demesne farm and the parish priest, who had an allocation of manor land to support himself, called the glebe, also had sections of the open fields.

Ploughing with oxen

The manorial system provided a means of cooperative management of the land, and, through the manor courts, a means of maintaining law and order within the community. Although most of the peasants were 'unfree' and tied to their land, they had a voice in the communal organisation of the local agriculture which was their livelihood.

There were traditionally two different manor courts, the Court Baron and the Court Leet. The View of Frankpledge was also held as part of the Court Leet. Although the Court Baron and Court Leet had different origins, they were normally combined and a joint court held twice a year. The Court Baron was directly concerned with manorial business and dealt with changes of tenancy, minor disputes between tenants and regulated the agricultural routine of the manor. The Court Leet was delegated to the manor by royal franchise and dealt with law and order. It had the power to deal with various offences and could fine or imprison offenders. The View of Frankpledge was an inspection of the tithings and was an extension of the Court Leet. A tithing was a group of ten households bound together with the mutual responsibility of maintaining law and order within the group. The head of the tithing, the tithing man, the forerunner of the village constable, was appointed at the View of Frankpledge[2].

Landholders in 1086

In 1086 large areas of land in the upper reaches of the Dun Valley belonged to Waleran, William I's huntsman, who held West Dean and part of East Dean for himself. Slightly further away he also held the manor of East Grimstead, the part of West Tytherley which was later to become Norman Court, Whaddon and land in King's Somborne, all of which were subinfeudated , or 'let out' to other, mainly Norman, estate holders. Waleran also had other estates further afield still and was a powerful landowner, a situation which must have seemed very different from the time before the conquest, when all the Dun Valley manors had been held individually by Saxon thegns. In contrast, land lower down the valley continued to be held by the Saxons who had been in possession in 1066; Alwi still held Lockerley, and also held East Tytherley, which his father had held previously, thereby providing considerable continuity for the local inhabitants.

The Domesday survey in 1086, which was carried out for taxation purposes, set out to compare the relative value of all the manors in both 1066 and 1086 by collecting the same information from each one. The area of land was assessed in hides and virgates, a hide being about 120 acres and a virgate,or yardland, 30 acres. A hide was considered to be the area which would support one family and their dependants for a year. These were therefore not accurate measurements of area, but an assessment which varied according to the quality of the land, and there was considerable regional variation in what constituted the area of a hide. The number of plough teams attached to a manor was recorded, as it was taken as an indication of arable productivity, likewise the number of villagers, who were classified according to their place in the feudal system. Woodland, pasture and meadow were assessed, and the number of mills and fishponds counted, all valuable assets which were part of the overall value of the manor. For example the Domesday survey records[3]:

West Dean manor

Waleran holds Dean himself. Godric held it before 1066;
it paid tax for 2 hides and 1 virgate of land. Land for 3 ploughs,
of which 1 hide is in lordship; 1 ½ ploughs there; 2 slaves;
1 villager and 10 cottagers with 1 ½ ploughs.
1 ½ mills which pay 16s; meadow 5 acres; woodland 1 furlong in both
length and width.
The value was and is 60s

East Grimstead

Herbert holds Grimstead from Waleran. Agemund held it before 1066;
it paid tax for 3 hides. Land for 3 ploughs, of which 1 ½ hides are in
lordship; 1 plough there; 2 slaves;
5 villagers and 7 cottagers with 3 ploughs.
Meadow 10 acres; woodland 5 furlongs long and 2 furlongs wide.
The value was and is 60s.

Under the Saxon kings many manors had been kept as part of the king's demesne lands and not given out to the Saxon noblemen, a system which continued under William the Conqueror. These royal manors were included in the Domesday survey, but did not have to pay tax to the king. Instead they owed him accommodation for a given number of nights each year for his court as the royal entourage progressed around the country. In west Hampshire, Broughton, Mottisfont, the Wallops and King's Somborne were all royal manors, and Broughton included land within the Dun Valley, as East Dean manor and Frenchmoor were both part of the manor of Broughton. East Dean parish was principally divided between this royal manor and an estate held by Waleran. In addition, there was a small area held by Herbert, a Norman who also had the manor of East Grimstead, which he leased from Waleran[4]. The Dun Valley was only a few miles south of the Roman road from Old Sarum to Winchester, at that time still a major highway, and so was within relatively easy reach of Winchester, the seat of power of the new regime.

Royal hunting forests

The change which probably had the greatest impact on the countryside following the Norman Conquest, particularly around Hampshire and south Wiltshire, was the creation of the royal forests. In Saxon times the kings had enjoyed hunting both for the sport and for the venison, and when staying in their demesne manors had ridden out in pursuit of the deer. During the winter months, when the only meat available was the preserved bacon and the salted beef or mutton, wild animals such as the deer and wild boar were a valuable source of fresh meat. There were not sufficient food resources to keep many farm animals over the winter, and most of them, except the essential breeding animals and the plough oxen, had to be slaughtered in the autumn, and the meat preserved by salting and smoking for the winter. Wild animals could feed themselves sufficiently on the countryside to survive.

The Saxon kings had always hunted within the boundaries of their own estates, but William I and his successors wanted to expand their sport into the wider countryside. This meant hunting across the estates held by their subjects, and to achieve this, whole regions were designated as hunting forests and subject to forest law. The land within the forest was still held by the barons and other landlords, but they were severely restricted in what they could do with it. Forest law protected not only the beasts of the chase, particularly the deer and the wild boar, but also the trees and vegetation

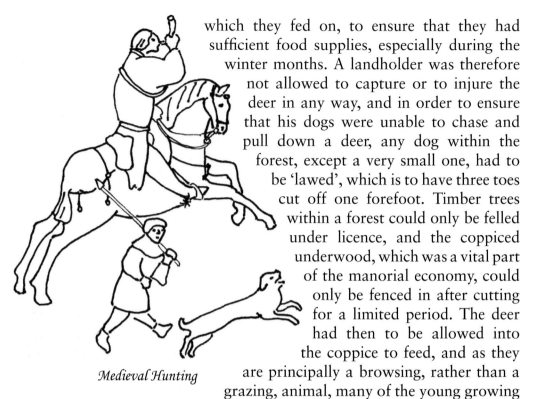

Medieval Hunting

which they fed on, to ensure that they had sufficient food supplies, especially during the winter months. A landholder was therefore not allowed to capture or to injure the deer in any way, and in order to ensure that his dogs were unable to chase and pull down a deer, any dog within the forest, except a very small one, had to be 'lawed', which is to have three toes cut off one forefoot. Timber trees within a forest could only be felled under licence, and the coppiced underwood, which was a vital part of the manorial economy, could only be fenced in after cutting for a limited period. The deer had then to be allowed into the coppice to feed, and as they are principally a browsing, rather than a grazing, animal, many of the young growing hazel shoots would have been eaten off. Coppice management depended on periodically cutting down all the hazel to ground level, after which the stools, or stumps, produced large numbers of young shoots, which would then be ready for harvesting several years later. Damage by deer eating the growing hazel would have been a major problem for the local villagers. Not surprisingly the royal forests of the Norman and Plantagenet kings were deeply unpopular, and caused considerable friction between the kings and their most powerful subjects, the barons.

The deer were principally fallow deer, which had been introduced into England by the Norman kings, but there were also the native roe and red deer. The prize quarry, which was reserved for the king, was the red deer stag. Wild boar were still plentiful around the woodland in the 11th and 12th centuries, but their numbers declined over subsequent centuries. They were present in small numbers in Britain until the 15th century, the last few probably interbreeding with the domestic pigs, which were also foraging around the woodland for at least part of the year. Hunting forests were usually created where there was a mixture of woodland and open country; 'forest' in this sense does not imply continuous woodland. These royal forests covered vast tracts of land throughout England, but Hampshire was particularly heavily afforested. They often utilized the areas of the English landscape which were less suitable for agriculture, and it was therefore a large tract of rather unproductive land in the Hampshire basin, within easy reach of Winchester, which was chosen for the creation of the 'new forest' in 1087. The bounds of the original New Forest extended much further northwards than they do today, and included the region which later became the separate forests of Clarendon, Buckholt and Melchet. The Dun Valley was well within the bounds of the original forest, and the first warden of the whole area was Waleran. From 1216 onwards the northern part became a separate group of royal forests based around the king's palace of Clarendon, and was administered by a separate warden. This group included the Clarendon and Melchet forests in Wiltshire, and Buckholt just over the county boundary in Hampshire. The boundaries of Clarendon Forest were formed by the county boundary in the east, the river Avon in the west, the Sarum to Winchester Roman road to the north and Dean Hill formed the southern boundary. Melchet was contiguous with Clarendon Forest, forming a common boundary along Dean Hill. Eastwards across the county boundary, beginning at West Dean, was Buckholt Forest, and the Dun Valley formed its southern boundary.

Royal hunting forests had a significance far beyond the king's sporting rights across the countryside, they were a status symbol for the Crown and the forest laws were a means of keeping the nobility in check. Not surprisingly, the nobility resented the control. Following the Norman Conquest the royal forests caused three centuries of strife between the kings and their most powerful subjects, the barons. Successive kings tried to extend the forest boundaries, but whenever the king needed money or cooperation from the barons, the latter tried to exert pressure to have the size of the forests reduced[5]. The boundaries of Clarendon therefore waxed and waned, so that Bentley Wood was not subject to forest law in 1225, but was within the boundaries of Clarendon in 1327[6]. Buckholt boundaries were also gradually contracted, and by 1300 the forest had become much reduced, so that it no longer extended down to the river Dun. By this time there were two bailiwicks, the east bailiwick which formed the later civil parish of Buckholt, while the west bailiwick was based around the later Norman Court and included West Tytherley village. Both Frenchmoor and East Tytherley manor were outside the forest bounds by 1300[7]. The royal forests continued to be a source of friction between the kings and their subjects until the middle of the 14th century, after which the problem gradually diminished. Royal forests still existed, but the forest laws were no longer strictly enforced.

Medieval manors in the Dun Valley parishes

The parish in medieval times was the community which supported a priest in a parish church, principally by the payment of tithes. Tithes, or the payment of one tenth of the annual produce of the land, were made obligatory in the 10th century, and the area which contributed to a particular church became its parish. The tithes went to the priest, thus providing him with an income, and he in return looked after the spiritual welfare of the parishioners. Some churches had their origins in the Saxon minster churches, but most parish churches were founded by estate owners in late Saxon and early Norman times, and the original parish often equated with the boundaries of one manor estate. In other cases there were several separate smaller estates all contributing to the one parish church[8]. Since the size and shape of parishes was originally determined by secular estate boundaries, it was the agricultural and other requirements of those estates which were ultimately the determining factors. Where estates had outlying areas of land, or had distant grazing rights, these became detachments of the parish. Maps of the Dun Valley drawn in the 19th century show many small detached parish areas; Lockerley and Broughton parishes both had three detachments (Ordnance Survey map first edition, surveyed 1870s).

West Dean and East Grimstead. Waleran the huntsman had a lasting influence on the medieval history of West Dean since he founded the dynasty which held the manor there. It seems likely that the mound at the top of Castle Hill was their fortified castle. Today it is just a tree-covered mound half hidden among woodland and modern houses, but in the 12th and 13th centuries it must have been an impressive stronghold, probably with a timber castle there. The position can be seen in the 1st ed. Ordnance Survey map (Fig. 3). G. S. Master, writing in 1885, describes the earth mound and disturbed land around it as a British camp, but there is no evidence for this. However, his comment that it was used as a bowling green in the early 19th century is likely to be correct, particularly as he was writing not too long afterwards, when it would have been a credible part of the local oral tradition. It was later described as a Norman motte and bailey[9] and is a scheduled monument (Wilts Scheduled Monument AM 312). More recent investigation suggests that while it is indeed a medieval fortified site, it was originally probably a ringwork rather than a motte, and that the mound was created during the post-medieval period from the outer banks[10]. As G. S. Master stated in the 19th century, it had been much altered to become a garden feature. In Norman times castles, the private

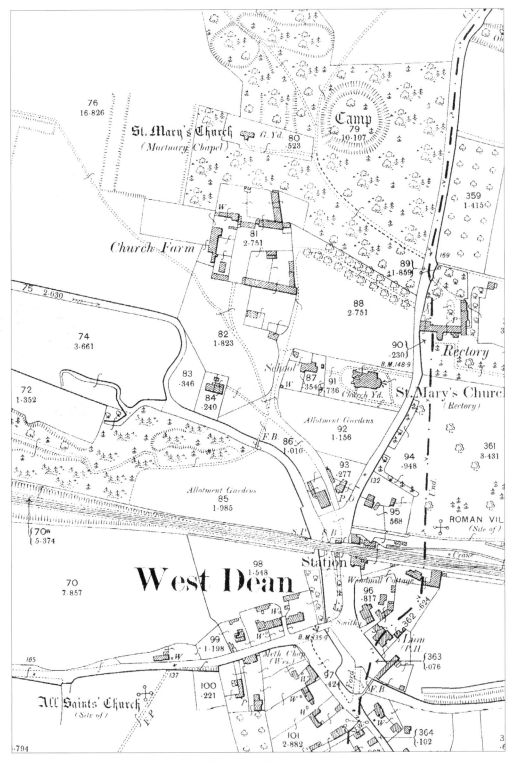

Fig. 3 *The Ordnance Survey map c 1900.*

fortified residences of great landowners, were a common feature of the landscape, not only in Britain but across France and other parts of Europe as well. Early castles from the late Saxon and early Norman period were usually wooden structures, defended by being placed on an earth motte (mound) often within an area enclosed by a bank and ditch (the bailey). There were also heavily embanked enclosures with defended entrances but without mottes, called ringworks, which would have had one or more timber buildings within the enclosure[11].

Waleran's descendants, the Walerand family, held the combined manor of West Dean and East Grimstead as well as the position of warden of the New Forest and Clarendon Forest until the death of Walter Walerand c 1200. His heirs were his three daughters, Cecelia, Albreda and Isabel, and his estates were divided between them, or rather between their husbands, as husbands took over their wives' inheritance. The Cecelia line died out when her son was executed and his estate forfeited in 1280-1, as a result of which it was subsequently divided between the families of the other two sisters. During the 13th century the West Dean estate was expanded by the addition of the southern fringe of Bentley Wood in 1227, a gift from Ela, Countess of Salisbury who held the manor of Amesbury (see below). This land had also been divided between the three sisters. The two lines continued separately until the middle of the 16th century, when they were re-united by the marriage of Sir John Harcourt, a descendant of Albreda, and Margaret, a descendant of Isabel. A simplified diagram of the family tree is given in chapter 4 and a full description of the descent of the Waleran family can be found in Colt Hoare (1837)[12] and Master (1885)[13]. The family tradition of holding the position of forest warden was continued for a further generation by the husbands of two of the Walerand sisters, Isabel and Cecilia[14].

Albreda married Sir John Ingham and their great-grandson was Sir Oliver Ingham who became a distinguished soldier and the governor of Marlborough, Devizes and other royal castles. He died in 1344 and his manor of West Dean and East Grimstead is described in his Inquisition Post Mortem[15] given below. These documents were records of the assets of the tenants-in-chief, who held land directly from the king, and were assessed after death by an inquisition so that the king could be given an accurate list.

Oliver de Ingham held of the king in chief in his demesne the manor of Westdeone and Estgrymstede by barony. In the said manor there is 1 messuage with garden and curtilages, 50 acres arable in severalty worth

12d/acre, 50 acres in the common field worth 8d/acre, 100 acres in the common field worth 1d/acre, 100 acres in the common field worth 1/2d/ acre, 30 acres meadow worth 2s/acre, 40 acres wood the pasture of which is worth 10s. There are £13 13s ½ d rents of assize. The pleas and perquisites of the courts are worth 30s/year.

Messuage: A house with its associated buildings

Rent of assize: Held at fixed rent

In addition to West Dean Ingham also had other manors, including Steeple Langford, which he held from the king, and the manor of Hamptworth, which belonged to the Bishop of Winchester. Some of his estates he let out to other landholders, including a manor in West Tytherley to Roger Norman which became the later Norman Court estate. Oliver Ingham's land was of course only half of the original Waleran estate.

At the death of Oliver Ingham his estate was subdivided between two daughters, as his only son had pre-deceased him. One of these daughters had already died, so that it was her daughter, Mary Curzon, who inherited along with her aunt Joan Lestrange. The details of the distribution of Oliver Ingham's West Dean estate in 1348 are interesting; two manor houses and their attached buildings are described, both of which appear to be in the vicinity of the ringwork.

Partition of the Lands of Oliver de Ingham (Wilts IPMs Edward III, 1348)[16]

1.   *To Roger le Strange, and Joan his wife, 1 grange, 1 longhouse with pigsty and a plot of ground inside the court, a garden on the south side, a moiety of la Castelhulle, 1 croft called Castelcroft, 3 ½ acres at la Hurne in Peykesbrouk.*

This moiety also included many small areas of land, presumably in the common fields, half of one sheepfold and the rents and services of about 20 people.

2 . *To Mary Curzon, Countess of Norfolk, daughter of John Curzon, 1 hall with chambers annexed, 1 kitchen, 1 longhouse from the gate towards the hall, a small garden bounding a piece of ground in the court. The moiety of la Castelhulle next to the hall, a small croft called Frerescroft, all the garden called Freresorchard.*

Croft: an enclosed area of land adjacent to a dwelling

There were also many small parcels of land as above, and the rents of 17 bond (unfree) tenants.

Castelhulle is recognisable as the modern Castle Hill in West Dean, and refers to the ringwork and the land surrounding it. For it to have been shared between the two estates suggests that it was still an important feature, even though it was no longer necessary to have a defensive castle in this part of England. Peykesbrook, or Pegsbrook as it has been called ever since, is an area in the southernmost part of Bentley Wood, and the name probably meant a 'picked' or pointed shaped coppice with a brook[17]. Frere, in Frerescroft, was a local surname, probably originally derived from Friar, and one of Mary Curzon's tenants was Richard Frere. Both houses had an enclosed garden, which may have been the small ornamental garden, or herber, typical of manor houses of that time, or a more utilitarian kitchen garden. An ornamental garden usually had a lawn surrounded by flowers and scented herbs, and a section for medicinal herbs, whereas kitchen gardens were stocked with food and medicinal plants. The vegetables grown in medieval times included various brassicas such as colewort and cabbage, root crops such as parsnips and turnips, leeks and some peas and beans. For decoration there were the modern cottage garden flowers such as roses, irises and peonies, while the medicinal plants and aromatic herbs were very similar to those available today[18].

It can only be speculation as to which of the two houses was the home of Oliver Ingham, and he must have been very much an absentee landlord, but Mary Curzon appears to have inherited the larger establishment. Only four years had elapsed since Oliver Ingham died, and the estate affairs had only just been settled, so that this house was probably already in existence. Fig. 4 is an attempted reconstruction of the ground plan of Mary Curzon's house, the site of which was adjacent to the ringwork. The absence of stone in the locality suggests that the buildings were timber and wattle-and-daub, with thatched roofs. A longhouse was a later development of the early medieval single-room dwelling, and had a passageway across the centre of the building which subdivided the space, with living rooms on one side and animal accommodation on the other, all under the same roof with a single entrance. In this case the longhouse may have been the earlier living accommodation. The hall, with its separate chambers and surrounding courtyard with gated entrance, was a relatively sophisticated

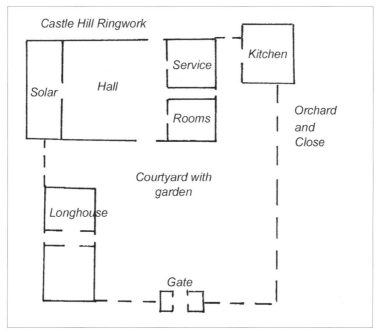

Castle Hill Ringwork

Solar | Hall

Service

Kitchen

Rooms

Orchard and Close

Longhouse

Courtyard with garden

Gate

Fig. 4 *A possible ground plan of Mary Curzon's manor buildings, West Dean, 1348.(MB)*

building in 1348. The subdivision of the hall into separate chambers was likely to have provided a solar, or private room for the lord of the manor and his family, and service rooms for food preparation and storage. The detached kitchen reduced the risk of fire spreading to the main building. The development of an enclosed courtyard with an entrance gate, which probably had a gatehouse, provided some protection from peasants with criminal intent[19].

Tragically, another event which happened in 1348 was to have a far greater impact on the local community around West Dean than changes on the estate. Plague, or the Black Death, first reached England during that year, entering the country from ships landing at ports along the south coast. *Yersinia pestis*, the bacterium causing the disease, was carried by fleas on rats and within a few months had spread throughout the country. The effects were catastrophic, affecting all levels of society, and whole communities died within a very short time during the outbreak. The death toll nationally has been estimated to have been about one third of the population. The situation was made worse by the fact that the country had been relatively over-populated in relation to its food supplies during the first part of the 14th century, and many of the poorer sections of society were also already weakened by famine, due to a period of bad harvests caused by a deterioration of the weather pattern. Further outbreaks of the plague occurred in 1361, 1369 and 1379, so that by 1400 the population was half what it had been in 1300[20].

Mary Curzon's ownership of her manor in West Dean was destined to be short-lived, since she was one of many deaths in 1349. There is no record of where she died, and as Countess of Norfolk it may not have been locally, but her Inquisition Post Mortem shows all too clearly that most of her tenants in West Dean and East Grimstead had also recently died.

Inquisition of Mary, wife of Stephen Tumby, 1349 (Wilts IPMs EdwardIII)[21]

Mary held in her demesne as of fee a moiety of the manor of West Dean and East Grimstead from the king in chief by barony.

A messuage, 150 acres arable land, 50 acres of which can be sown each year, 50 acres lies fallow and the pasture (of the fallow) *is worth nil because they lie in common. 7 acres meadow, which after mowing lies in common, in dry summers they cannot be mown. 60 acres oakwood in which there is no underwood at present, nor any pasture* (of the woodland) *because they lie in common. Rents from the lands of Geoffrey de Weston, John Hulon and Cicely Quentes, free tenants. Not from John Andrew, Walter Wodekok, Stephen Thomas, John Kerde, Richard le Frere, Clarice Dodde and Thomas le Tannere, tenants who held tenements at certain rents but are now dead, all the tenements are in the king's hands and are worth nothing, unoccupied and had deteriorated before they could be sold for want of buyers.*

Also William le Haneker, John Pompe, Edmund Saleman, John Wherwe and John Gerde the younger, bond tenants likewise dead and all these tenements are in the king's hands because of the death of Mary. Joan, wife of Roger Lestrange, aunt of Mary, is the next heir.

At that time all the manor tenants had common pasture rights in both the arable fallow and in the woodland at certain times of the year, which reduced their value to the lord of the manor. The villages had obviously been devastated by plague; the above document deals only with the heads of the households, but many of their families would have been wiped out as well. This inquisition implies that the houses had already deteriorated, demonstrating just how quickly general decay happens in such circumstances, and if the crops were not harvested and the ground not tilled, a wilderness would very soon have developed. Many farm animals must have wandered off and fended for themselves, or been taken over by anyone who was still alive. During the years which followed the whole face of the Dun Valley countryside would have changed, with former arable fields becoming wasteland with scrub, the river choked with weed, and the neatly coppiced woodland overgrown. West Dean and East Grimstead are well documented because of this Inquisition, but many other villages around must have suffered the same fate. However the local villages survived, and none of the Dun Valley communities were lost completely, as happened in some areas.

The two halves of the original Waleran estate continued as separate manors until the 16th century, when they were re-united by the marriage of Sir John Harcourt and Margaret Barentyne. It was once again all within a single family, and it remained so until the manor was sold to George Evelyn in 1618[22].

Waleran had not held the whole of West Dean parish in 1086, since the parish also included Bentley Wood, the woodland which extended north of the village almost as far as the village of Winterslow, and as far eastwards as the county boundary. In the Domesday survey this stretch of woodland was part of the 29,000 acres of woodland owned by the royal manor of Amesbury, which had previously belonged to the Saxon kings. No details are given in the survey but it is thought that the Amesbury woodland included the whole Clarendon area. The manor passed from the Crown to the Earl of Salisbury in the 1140s, and at that time most of the woodland was separated from Amesbury manor. Bentley Wood, however, remained as part of the manor estate, since there was very little woodland around Amesbury and to be a viable estate a manor needed a source of wood. Throughout the centuries which followed, a large part of Bentley Wood remained attached to Amesbury manor.

During the early 13th century the Earl of Salisbury was William Longespee, an illegitimate son of the king, Henry II. Longespee had extensive plans to build a monastery in the southern part of Bentley Wood, and he made a clearing for it in the woodland. Unfortunately he died before building work had commenced, and his widow Ela, Countess of Salisbury, preferred a site at Lacock, another of her estates, for the monastery, and she eventually founded an abbey there. The land in the southern part of Bentley Wood which was to have been the monastery site, Ela gave as an endowment to St. Nicholas's Hospital, an almshouse in Salisbury which was to house twelve needy old people and provide aid to others. This part of the wood, which became known as Howe Farm, was leased out and the revenue it brought in was used to provide for the poor people in the almshouse. Both the tenants of Howe Farm and St Nicholas's Hospital itself had common rights of grazing for their animals, not only in the southern part of Bentley Wood, but also throughout the part which still belonged to Amesbury manor. Another institution which also benefited from common rights in Bentley Wood was Amesbury Priory, which had rights of pannage there for 100 pigs during the autumn, and the right to take one cartload of wood a day from the woodland. These rights, along with similar rights elsewhere, had been granted to the priory when it was founded by king Henry II in the 12th century. Ela, Countess of Salisbury, also gave the southern fringe of Bentley Wood to the West Dean estate, to the husbands of the three Walerand sisters[23].

East Tytherley. Downstream from West Dean the largest manor which was not a royal manor was East Tytherley. The Domesday survey[24] assessed that it had been worth 60s in 1066, and therefore very similar in value and status to West Dean and East Grimstead. By 1086 it was worth only 40s; possibly its Saxon landlord had lost land to the new Norman nobility.

Alwi the son of Saulf holds Tederleg of the king. His father held it as an alod (freehold). *Then, as now, it paid geld for 3 hides. There is land for 4 ploughs. In demesne are 2 ploughs; and 2 villeins and 9 bordars with 2 ploughs. There are 2 mills worth 27s 6d, and 27 acres of meadow. There is woodland worth 30 swine. It was worth 60s; it is now worth 40s.*

It is difficult to make a meaningful comparison of the extent of woodland between different manors at that time as it was sometimes measured in furlongs, and sometimes by the number of pigs which it would support.

In Lockerley there were two much smaller manors, one held by Ulvric worth 5s and one held by Alwi worth 30d.

Towards the end of the 12th century East Tytherley manor was held by the Columbars, an influential Norman family from Colombieres in Normandy, and who were hereditary cup-bearers to the Crown. Thomas de Columbars was the first to hold East Tytherley manor, followed by Michael and then Matthew, who were thought to have been his son and grandson[25]. East Tytherley at that time included Holbury, East Dean, Lockerley and Broughton as adjoining members, making it an extensive land holding. Michael de Columbars and his son Michael were also hereditary wardens of the royal forest of Chute, which was partly in Hampshire and partly in Wiltshire, extending northward from Clarendon and Buckholt.

Hunting for sport, and keeping deer as a source of venison, may have been the pastime of kings, but the nobility were able to indulge in a more limited version in the form of deer parks. As deer were held to be the property of the king, permission was legally required to enclose a park, and if the manor was within the bounds of a royal forest a release from forest law for the area of the park was essential. Many deer parks were created throughout the country during the 12th and 13th centuries, and the number of parks reached a peak during the latter half of the 13th century. At this time the royal hunting forest of Buckholt extended from the Buckholt hills down to the river Dun, and East Tytherley was therefore subject to forest law. However, the Columbars wanted to follow the trend, and it was Michael de Columbars who first enclosed the park around the manor of East Tytherley with a 'dike and hedge'. In 1245 Matthew, his son, paid 100 marks to enable him to keep the enclosure. This appears to have been a retrospective application for a licence to empark, a not uncommon practice at that time. The licensing of parks provided welcome revenue for the Crown, so that even in the royal forests it was not particularly discouraged. In 1248 another of the Columbars, Peter de Columbars, was granted permission to have a park in Somerset, which was known to have been already enclosed by 1222[26]. Matthew de Columbars must have found favour with the king because in 1270 he was rewarded for good service[27]:

Grant to Matthew de Columbaris and his heirs for good service, to be quit of lawing dogs within the manor of Tytherley and its members Lockerlie and Holebiry which are within the mete and regard of Buckholt.

The deerpark.

Parks were usually enclosed with a bank on top of which was a wooden paling fence. On the inside of the bank there was a ditch, the soil from which would have been used to construct the bank, and the whole structure had to be high and wide so that the deer could not jump out. The bank which surrounded East Tytherley park is still clearly visible today in places (Fig.III, p8). The most commonly kept species of deer was the fallow, which normally live in large groups or herds, and adapt easily to the confined conditions of the park. Red or roe deer were sometimes kept as well, although the different species had to be kept separately, as they do not mix very well when closely confined. At the nearby manor of King's Somborne there were two separate parks, so that both red and fallow deer could be kept. The enclosed parks were a much more efficient means of producing venison than hunting wild deer across the countryside, and even the kings with their love of the chase across the forest also had parks.

The park was usually a mixture of open areas or 'launds', and woodland, which provided a suitable environment for keeping large numbers of deer, and for hunting them within the park. Parks were also used as a source of timber trees, and could produce smaller diameter wood from enclosed coppice areas within the park, or from pollarded trees. A pollard is a tree cut back to a stump several feet high, which sprouts many branches from that point, providing a source of young wood too high for the deer to reach and damage. Providing that the open areas were not over-grazed, cattle and pigs could also be kept in the park, which meant that the land was more productive. Another common feature of medieval deer parks was the fishpond, and local streams were frequently diverted to create a pond so that it could be stocked with fish such as pike, eels, tench, roach and carp for the manor kitchen, as well as providing a source of water for the deer[28]. The fishpond in East Tytherley park can still be seen today, albeit rather overgrown. Pheasants, partridge and hares were also often kept within parks, and not infrequently there was a coneygre, or rabbit warren. Rabbits were not native to the British Isles, but were introduced by the Normans as a useful food source. Unlike rabbits today, they were not originally well-adapted to their environment, and had to be provided with mounds of soft soil or sand in which to dig their burrows. From the list of species which thieves removed on one occasion in 1374, East Tytherley park was used for keeping game birds and also had a warren[29]:

Commission of oyer and terminer to John de Foxle, Peter ate Wode and William de Houghton, touching evildoers who broke into the king's park and entered his free warren at Tudderleye, county Southampton. Hunting in these and carried away deer from the park, and from the warren into which they had been driven, and hares, pheasants and partridge from the warren.

Oyer and (de)terminer: 'hear and decide', the hearing of a case in court.

Later lords of the manor of East Tytherley during medieval times include Queen Philippa, the wife of Edward III, who held the manor from 1335 – 69. She is unlikely to have spent much, or any, time there, and for some of the years at least appointed keepers or guardians to take care of the estate. The Rolls of Patent Records in 1353, 1354 and 1357 include orders to keepers to make surveys of the manor and to carry out extensive repairs. In the 1350s it is likely that the manor was in a poor state of repair after a prolonged period of minimal maintenance during the years which followed the plague epidemic of 1348-9[30]:

Appointment of Peter de Brugge and William de Putton, guardian of Queen Philippa's manor of Tiderle, to take as many workmen, artificers and servants, not in the king's service, as are required for her works at Tiderle, and to put them to work there at her wages to be paid according to the form of the late statute touching such servants.

In 1391-2 the fabric of the manor was still in a poor state and the king, Richard II, ordered the keepers to carry out repairs to *'the dilapidated chamber called La Blanchechambre and an old chapel there'*. The lead-roofed chambers of the gate-house were also to be renovated. East Tytherley manor was an extensive establishment of several buildings within an enclosed courtyard, and there were also farm buildings on the site. The repair work was to be financed by the sale of *'beeches large and small growing in the woods called les Thornes and la Quenewode to the sum of 100s'*[31,32]. Not surprisingly the manor was still referred to as Queencourt in the mid-15th century, and in the 19th century a piece of land along the river bank in Lockerley was still called Queenmead, while the northern part of East Tytherley parish included Queenwood and Queenwood Down.

In 1496 George Bainbridge was granted the manor of East Tytherley[33], which included part of Lockerley parish. Bainbridge had already been granted the manor of Lockerley Butler in 1493, and from that time onwards the manors were combined. Lockerley Butler was named after John le Boteler who held it in 1293.

Lockerley. The history of the parish of Lockerley is closely interwoven with that of East Tytherley[34]. Although in some cases a manor included the whole parish, and often followed the parish boundaries, this was not always so, and both Lockerley and East Dean parishes contained more than one manor. In the Domesday survey Lockerley was described as a member of East Tytherley manor, and later on during the 13th century under the Columbars, East Tytherley manor had extended well into Lockerley parish. The close association of the two parishes was made even closer when the manors of Lockerley Butler and East Tytherley were combined under George Bainbridge. However, in addition to these two manors there were various other small manor estates within the parish of Lockerley. Some of these areas of land later combined with bigger estates, whereas others became separated away from larger holdings. Such transfers often came about because land held directly from the king by a major landholder reverted to the Crown on his death, and while it was usually passed to the next heir, where there was no direct next of kin the land was taken back into the king's hands. It was then granted by the king to someone else.

One small manor in Lockerley belonged to the Columbars, who already held the manor of East Tytherley. It was for this manor that Matthew Columbar was granted a charter in about 1271 to hold a weekly market and an annual fair there[35]. This was not just a way of enabling the local villagers to buy and sell their produce more easily, it was also a business opportunity for the Columbars. The lord of the manor paid the Crown for a charter to hold a market or fair, but he in turn then exacted tolls from the market traders. This manor only remained associated with the manor

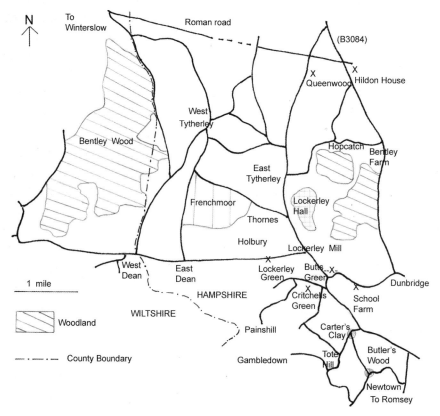

Fig. 5 *The Dun Valley to show places mentioned in the text.(MB)*

of East Tytherley until the early 14th century, when it was granted to John de Vienna and became part of East Dean manor.

Another way in which land boundaries were sometimes redrawn was by grants from landholders to the church, or to religious houses. The priory of St. Denys, Southampton, acquired a manor estate in Lockerley in this manner when various pieces of land there were donated to the priory during the 13th century. The Columbars gave a half share in the mill on the Lockerley Mill site, and land nearby was also granted to the priory by other landholders (see chap 5). Two other small estates, which existed in Lockerley in medieval times, remained as separate entities and never became part of the manor of East Tytherley and Lockerley. Their detailed history is somewhat obscure but they probably became the present day Gambledown and Painshill farms[36].

East Dean. There were two principal manors in East Dean, one of which had been a member of the royal manor of Broughton in 1086. Following a succession of landholders it was granted at the beginning of the 14th century to John de Vienna and his wife, who were also granted both the small manor in Lockerley which had belonged to the Columbars (see above) and Holbury manor at about the same time. Holbury had been part of the manor of East Tytherley under the Columbars[37]. John de Vienna had been appointed warden of the royal hunting forest of Clarendon in 1291[38], a position which by this time had acquired considerable profits and perquisites. The list of what John de Vienna was able to claim is not known but was probably very similar to that of Roger de Mortuo Mari, the Earl of March, who was warden in 1355[39]. His perquisites included large quantities of wood, a valuable asset in those days, the nut crop throughout the bailiwick (Clarendon only and not associated forests), unclaimed stray animals, the profits from certain meadows for the sustenance of his horses and other livestock, tolls to be exacted from people carrying goods across the forest, and as a heriot when a forester died, his best riding horse and its equipment, his horn, bow and arrow and hunting dog. However, it has to be remembered that officials did not receive salaries as they would today, and this was an effective way of making the local community provide him with the money and goods in kind.

This manor of East Dean became attached to the manor of West Tytherley during the 14th century. In 1486 it was united with the manor of Norman Court[40], which meant that from that time onwards Norman Court held land in the Dun Valley, and along the banks of the river Dun.

The other manor of East Dean belonged to Mottisfont priory (see chap. 5) and was known to have been held by the prior in 1361. It remained with the priory until the dissolution of the monasteries, after which the buildings and land were granted to William, Lord Sandys, and East Dean was then part of the manor of Mottisfont. A further estate in East Dean was the land which Waleran had held there at the Domesday survey. It was donated to Salisbury Cathedral by Walter Walerand towards the end of the 12th century, after which it remained in the hands of the dean and chapter until 1880. This ownership was not quite continuous as such ecclesiastical lands were disposed of during the Commonwealth, but it was restored to the dean and chapter following the accession of Charles II[41].

Kimbridge. Now part of the parish of Mottisfont, Kimbridge manor was held in the 13th century by Michael de Kimbridge, and the descent of the manor as far as it is known is covered by the VCHH (vol 4 p508). The manor was held by the Canterton family from the 15th until the early 17th centuries as part of the manor of East Tytherley, and Kimbridge was represented as a tything in the East Tytherley manor court rolls. William Canterton's probate inventory is included in Chapter 6, and it shows an interesting link with the past, as one of his horses was named Fish, presumably bought from a man named Fish. The Fish family had been heirs to the manor in 1412-13, although they do not appear to have held it, and their descendants were presumably still around in the area 150 years later.

Dunbridge. Also part of Mottisfont parish, the manor was held in conjunction with Pittleworth in Bossington parish. The location of the manor buildings was on the site where Dunbridge Farm now stands, on the Lockerley to Dunbridge road[42].

Frenchmoor. This was the land which formed a detachment of Broughton parish on the northern edge of the Dun Valley and was part of the manor of Broughton in the 13th century. Originally it may well have been held as a valuable outlying stretch of woodland or grazing land for the manor. Geographically it lay sandwiched between areas of Norman Court land from the 15th century onwards, with West Tytherley to the north and their East Dean estate to the south. During the mid 17th century Broughton manor became the property of Sir John Evelyn, so that in the 17th and 18th centuries Frenchmoor would have been closely associated with West Dean.

3
The Landscape

Many aspects of the countryside in and around the Dun Valley were very similar in the past to its appearance today. Since man first settled there in appreciable numbers, it has been a managed landscape, composed of woodland, open countryside and fields, and while the proportions have varied over the centuries, the essential ingredients remain the same. The soil type and the nature of the terrain have always played a major part in determining which areas of land were used for which purposes, the best valley soils being used for hay meadows, while the heavy badly-drained clay was left as woodland, and sheep grazed on the steep chalk hillside of Dean Hill. A steep rise in the population changed this towards the end of the 13th century, when the cultivated arable fields were pushed ever higher up onto the poorer soils and steeper hillsides. These areas were then abandoned when the population fell dramatically in the 14th century, after which the proportion of land used for agriculture then gradually increased, taking into cultivation some of the rough grazing and woodland. The river would have looked very much as it looks today, and was utilised by the inhabitants of the villages along the valley. The volume of water flowing down the river must have varied with the rainfall, and been affected by both long-term climate changes and normal seasonal variation. The extent of modern water extraction in the whole region has probably had an effect on current levels, but there has not been a very dramatic change in the size of the river during the last millennium.

Agriculture

The open field system described in Chapter 2 was the principal method of producing corn crops in all the Dun Valley parishes until it was gradually replaced by enclosure and the formation of separately-managed farms, and large areas continued to be farmed cooperatively in open fields until the 19th century. Since general enclosure of parishes occurred at about the same time as the Tithe Commutation Act 1836, the tithe maps show the land as very recently enclosed. The newly-formed fields, allocated as allotments at enclosure, were often collections of the individual strips in the old furlongs which the farmers had previously cultivated. These new fields were often named after the open fields, and the location of the old common fields can therefore often be established. Enclosure maps and estate maps of around the late 18th and early 19th centuries also often show a similar connection between the new and old fields.

A map of East Dean from 1830[1], while showing the post-enclosure landscape, marks the old open field names across it , so that their position between the valley road and Dean Hill can be seen quite clearly. The tithe map of East Dean includes fields called Allotment in East Field, Allotment in West Field and Allotment in Middle Field, confirming the names given in the 1830 map (Fig. 24). Field names are not always quite as obvious as this example, but the rectangular shape of recently enclosed fields on tithe or enclosure maps is also a useful guide. The enclosure map of East Grimstead shows how the common arable fields were divided up following the old strips and furlongs (Fig.IV, p9).

Large areas of each parish were devoted to providing common grazing for the cattle, sheep and horses, and this was often on the clay land north of the

Fig. 6 *Detail from East Grimstead tithe map showing former common land.(MB)*

river, away from the better river valley soil. Both East Grimstead and West Dean have such areas, where the names on the enclosure and tithe maps indicate that they were formerly common pasture. Fig. 6 shows the area which had been East Grimstead Common until it was enclosed in 1723 by agreement between Evelyn Pierrepont, Duke of Kingston, who was then lord of the manor, and his tenants[2]. The poor thin soil on the downland was also used for grazing, Queenwood Down in the northern part of East Tytherley was one such area, and along the valley the steeper parts of Dean Hill also provided similar grazing land.

Rabbit Warrens

When the appearance of the countryside in the past is compared with how it looks today, one difference is the presence of rabbits. Today they are one of our most commonly seen wild mammals, which are to be found in fields, hedgerows and on the roadsides everywhere. In the past this was not so; until the 19th century there were very few rabbits in the wild, whereas farming them in warrens was a widespread agricultural practice, and many manor estates would have had a warren.

Rabbits were introduced into Britain by the Normans, and the earliest records of them were in the 1230s. More locally they were recorded in Grovely Forest in 1285[3]. Originally rabbits were ill-adapted to our climate and conditions, and they were managed in large enclosures many acres in extent termed coneygars, or warrens, and provided with banks of loose earth in which to make their burrows. Rabbits breed rapidly and grow quickly, and they can be kept on poor quality land, particularly steep downland, which meant that an otherwise unproductive part of the estate could produce large quantities of meat. Grassland alone could not support the rabbits and extra food had to be provided, so various crops were grown in the enclosure including turnips, sow-thistle and dandelions. Hay was often provided during the winter[4]. A bank was usually thrown up around the warren to protect the rabbits from predators and to prevent escapes. As the rabbits gradually became better adapted to British conditions, the escaped animals learned to thrive and multiply in the wild, to the detriment of the crops on the surrounding land. Catching the rabbits in the warrens was carried out with ferrets and nets, sometimes assisted by dogs.

The field names on the tithe maps of the Dun Valley suggest that warrens had previously been a common feature of the local countryside. They also give the location. Lockerley had a Warren Field on the southern side of the Romsey road, a field in East Dean parish on Dean Hill was called Conegar and West Dean had fields called Coneygre and Little Coneygre to the east of Frenchmoor Lane. Augustine Stevens's accounts (chap. 8) for the manor of East Tytherley in 1680 include:

Paid William Matthews the warrener as for rabbits as by his bill appears £2 7s 6d

Woodland and Wood-Pasture

Much of the region around the Dun valley has always been heavily wooded, in contrast to the chalk downland regions of both Wiltshire and Hampshire. However, before the 18th century woods were not the dense blocks of plantation woodland with which we are so familiar today. Trees grew by natural regeneration, and wooded landscapes in the past were more similar to the general appearance of the present New Forest. There were extensive areas of wood-pasture, which provided grazing for farm animals and the deer, interspersed with woodland managed for wood production. Bentley Wood was known to have been a mixture of woodland with open areas of wet marshy grazing land[5], and other woodland further along the valley, as well as woods in East Tytherley at a greater distance from the river, must have been very similar.

When animals, both farm livestock and the wild deer, were roaming freely around woodland they would have eaten the new young shoots on the newly-cut trees unless measures were taken to prevent them from doing so. The small-diameter wood, as opposed to timber trees, was therefore produced either in coppices which were fenced in until the new growth had reached a good height, or as pollarded trees on the open pasture.

When many species of deciduous trees are cut down to just above ground-level, they produce multiple new shoots from the stump, or stool, which, after several years' growth, can be harvested as a crop of stems. The coppice stool remains in the ground and produces more shoots, gradually expanding with each harvesting cycle (Fig.VI, p43). Although the coppice has to be protected while the young shoots are growing, it is a very efficient and sustainable way of producing a continuous supply of small-diameter wood. Many tree species can be coppiced, but locally much of the coppice was hazel, which was used extensively for hurdle fences and as wattle-and-daub for buildings. Timber trees were grown among the coppice stools, provided that they were not so dense that the shade from their canopy kept the light from the 'underwood' layer of hazel below. The timber trees were produced by allowing naturally-grown saplings to become mature trees, instead of coppicing them at frequent intervals. Around the Dun Valley most of the timber trees were oak, which grows particularly well on the heavier soils, but there was some ash, elm, beech and the evergreen yew as well. Oak was the favoured wood for building construction as it has good durability for external use. It was usually cut after about 70 years' growth, when it had reached the right size for beams and supporting timber in buildings. Before mechanization timber was sawn by hand, and trees were cut down when they were the size required for a particular purpose to minimise the work. Timber was also not cut square and was often used with the bark still attached, for the same reason[6]. Beech was used for internal fittings such as furniture and panelling as it was a hard dense timber which could be carved easily and bent into shape. Extensive beech woods covered the Buckholt Hills north of the Dun Valley[7].

Mature trees also grew on the open pasture land, as well as along the roadsides and in hedgerows. Many of these were pollarded, or periodically cut back to a stump several feet high. A large number of branches then grew at the top of the stump, well above the browsing height of any animals grazing in the vicinity, and could be harvested when they reached the required size (Fig. VII, p43). Traditionally the branches of pollards belonged to the tenants on an estate, the tree trunk, which as it grew became valuable as timber, belonged to the lord of the manor. Pollarded trees would therefore have been a familiar sight in the local landscape in the past. They can reach a considerable size, but when pollards are repeatedly cut, they eventually run out of the epicormic buds which produce the new shoots, and the tree then dies. Pollarding was discouraged in the 17th and 18th centuries, because although it was a very useful source of wood for the villagers, it prevented trees growing on to produce timber, which did not suit the lord of the manor. Until the 20th century there was an almost inexhaustible requirement for wood of all sizes, and trees were constantly being cut and utilized. It was always tempting to cut trees as coppice or pollards for immediate use, rather than leave then untouched for generations to produce timber. As a consequence, one noticeable difference between the countryside of the past and its appearance today was that there would have been far fewer majestic old mature trees than we currently see along the hedgerows. However, a few managed to escape the axe, and particularly where a tree marked a boundary, it was allowed to remain intact and became a venerable old landmark tree, often acquiring a name. There was a notable beech tree at the crossroads of two major tracks in Bentley Wood, which is marked on large-scale first edition Ordnance Survey maps as Marigold Beech. Also within Bentley Wood, the present-day Pheru (originally Fair Yew) Coppice must have had a landmark yew tree at some distant point in history. The earliest record of the name is in 1540, showing that the names often outlive the trees[8].

The level of population in the area affected the woodland as well as the agricultural land. Increased population resulted in more woodland being cleared for arable land, and the woods and hedgerows being heavily cut to provide adequate supplies of wood for all sections of society. In contrast, when the population fell, particularly after the Black Death, coppices would have looked overgrown and there would have been more mature trees around the countryside. Reduced grazing of the open areas, as well as neglect of the arable fields, would have soon resulted in the landscape being invaded by brambles, hawthorn and other scrub bushes and trees.

The River

One obvious feature of the valley scenery is the River Dun, which increases noticeably in size as it flows along the valley, collecting water from all the springs and streams which run into it, until it in turn flows into the Test. Before the industrial revolution rivers were an invaluable source of power as well as water, and water mills were a common feature of many river valleys.

Mills on the river Dun. Manors situated in the Dun Valley which had access to the river bank had the benefit of being able to channel the water through a mill. The use of water power to grind corn was originally introduced into Britain by the Romans, but only a few Roman mill sites around the country have been identified. The Anglo-Saxons had water mills, and there is an increasing number of references to mills in charters and place-names from the 9th century onwards. Simple horizontal-wheeled mills existed at the same time as those with vertical wheels, and it is likely that earlier horizontal waterwheels were gradually replaced by vertical-wheeled mills. The greatest density of mills recorded in the Domesday survey was in central-southern England. During the 12th century windmills were introduced as an alternative to water power, the earliest form being the postmill supported in a mound of earth[9].

According to the Domesday survey, by 1066 the grinding of corn in water mills by the Saxons was well established. The survey gives the number of mills owned by the Saxons in 1066, the number in 1086, which manor they belonged to and their value. Unfortunately it does not give the exact location, and some mills were shared between two or more people or by adjoining villages. A 'mill' at that time implied a pair of millstones, so that where the description is two mills it is likely to mean two pairs of millstones, not necessarily two completely separate buildings. One waterwheel could only turn one pair of stones, so that not infrequently there were two milling units under one roof and using the same watercourse, each composed of a waterwheel and a pair of stones.

Mills were present on the river Dun by 1066, and may well have been there for many centuries previously. Waleran held 1 ½ mills at West Dean, which seems to be the furthest point upstream that the water flow was adequate to operate a waterwheel. A water-powered mill was an obvious asset, but if the water supply was only sufficient during part of the year, it might not have been worth the expenditure involved in the initial construction of a mill, and its subsequent maintenance. West Dean must have been rather marginal, because although there are a few references after 1086, there is no mention of a water mill there after the 14th century.

In 1201 – 03 Albreda Waleran held a third part of a mill in West Dean[10], showing that the mill was shared between the estates of the three sisters when their father's manor was divided between them (see chap. 4). The Bishop of Winchester held part of the manor of West Dean in 1352, probably for a limited period, and although he only had a third part of the garden, he appears to have had the whole mill[11]. This would, of course, have been not many years after the devastation of the plague epidemic, and it is interesting to speculate as to what condition the mill would have been in. To have been listed with the contents of the estate it must have been considered viable, but this is the last date at which there is any record of a water mill in West Dean.

Both East Tytherley manor and the manor of East Dean, which was attached to the royal manor of Broughton, had mills in 1086, according to the Domesday survey. In each case it was '2 mills', which as explained above could have meant one mill site in each case. There do appear to have been two separate mills in East Tytherley, and they were probably on the sites of the later Holbury and Lockerley mills and there is a fairly continuous record for each. In 1326 Richard Smerk held a water mill in *'Holeburi in Estuderle'* together with 60 acres of arable, 7 acres meadow, 3 acres underwood and 1 ½ acres of moor[12]. The site of Lockerley mill was within East Tytherley manor, and in the late 12th or early 13th centuries Thomas Columbars granted a moiety of that mill to the canons of St. Denys priory, Southampton (see chap. 5).

When the owners of manor estates first constructed mills to grind the corn, they managed them directly, employing a miller, and charged their tenants to have their corn ground. The natural progression from this was for the mill to be leased to the miller, who paid for the lease of the mill, but who then had control over its operation, and charged for grinding the corn. Millers were noted for being somewhat unscrupulous in their dealings with other manor tenants, and some local problems are described in Chapter 7. There are many records of leases of Holbury and Lockerley (Ford) mills during the 17th and 18th centuries, and the mills are also included in conveyancy agreements when the manor of East Tytherley and Lockerley changed hands. Such documents often list what buildings and land accompany the mill, but give few details about the mill itself.

Holbury Mill was situated on the parish boundary between East Dean, Lockerley and East Tytherley, and had land in all three parishes. The mill was owned as part of East Tytherley manor in the 17th century, and an 11 year lease from Dame Priscilla Rolle to James Spragge, miller, in 1689[13] records the following:

A grist (corn) water mill and mill (2 mills under 1 roof), in East Dean called Holbery Mill. It includes all buildings, orchards, gardens, millstone wheels and inplements, 1 close of meadow called Mill Mead (4 acres), 4 closes of arable, meadow and pasture called Horse Close (2 acres), 1 parcel of arable ground called Sandhille (6 acres) formerly part of Campione tenement.

All of which said premises lie in East Dean, East Tytherley and Lockerley, and are part of the manor of East Tytherley and Lockerley and were late in the tenure of Jane Spragge (James's mother).

To allow ingress, egress and regress to Priscilla Rolle. Timber rights are reserved, including all trees likely to grow into timber trees (oak, ash, elm, beech). She retains the right to create a grate or anything else for feeding, keeping and preserving fish for her use. Spragge was allowed to fish in the residue of the mill pond.

The mill on the site where St. Denys Priory had had their mill and surrounding estate, became Ford, and then Lockerley, mill in later centuries. In the 17th century it was part of the manor of East Tytherley and Lockerley, and is described in a conveyance of the manor in 1654[14] as follows:

Ford Mill (water corn mill) and 1 parcel of meadow called the More adjoining, with dovecote thereupon erected, 1 hop garden on an island lying near the bridge that leads from Ford to Lockerley, buildings, barns, stables, gardens, orchards, woods, wears, water courses, ponds, pools, fishings and flood hatches.

There are no records of a mill in East Dean after the Domesday survey, and it may have been that Holbury was the furthest point upstream that could sustain a water mill under all conditions over the centuries. Norman Court manor held land along the river bank in East Dean, and as there is no river in West Tytherley successive lords of the manor must have at least considered the idea of a mill on the Dun. However, carting grain long distances to a water mill would have been a major disadvantage, particularly as the economics of the mill depended on forcing every copyhold tenant to make use of it, and a windmill might have seemed a more attractive option. Mills, whether they used water or wind power, were built by the lord of the manor, who then charged his tenants for using it. It was compulsory for them to have their corn ground there, even when it would have been easier and cheaper for them to have done it themselves with a hand-mill.

In 1256 the warden of Clarendon was ordered to supply one mill post and five timber oaks to the sister of John Mauncell, treasurer of York, who held the manor of Broughton. The wood was for a windmill in Tytherley, probably West Tytherley[15], which must have seemed a very new idea at the time since windmills had only appeared in Britain in the late 12th or early 13th century. Unfortunately there are no later records of a windmill operating in West Tytherley.

There are the archaeological remains of windmills on the southern side of Dean Hill, another area without easy access to a river for water mills, whereas the only record of a windmill in the Dun Valley itself is in West Dean. Master, writing in 1885, records that there was a windmill and malthouse adjacent to the railway station, which had been purchased from Augustine Cooper in 1733, but gives no indication of its age[16]. Presumably wind power was more reliable than using the river so far upstream.

4
The Lords of the Manor

A detailed description of the descent of all the manors and smaller estates in the Dun Valley over a thousand-year period is outside the scope of this book, but much of what is known is covered by the VCHH 4, which also includes the manor of West Dean and East Grimstead, although they lie over the county boundary. Both G.S. Master and Richard Colt Hoare also give further information on West Dean[1,2]. However, the lord of the manor played such an important part in the history of the villages and estate communities, a few individuals more than others, that some information about the families who lived in the manor houses is an integral part of the Dun Valley history. Although the lord of the manor was the most important member of the community, he was often a distant figure who held other estates, and was not constantly present in person in the manor house, leaving the manor steward to manage the day-to-day affairs around the estate. The lineage of the families is made more difficult by the frequent use of the same Christian names in succeeding generations, and as not all the successive holders of a manor are of particular interest, the following information on the more important families is given in an abbreviated form to provide an easy reference for other sections of the history of the Dun Valley.   (d = died, m = married).

Waleran

The Waleran, later named Walerand, dynasty were descendants of Waleran the hunter who held West Dean and East Grimstead at the time of the Domesday survey, together with extensive lands in the rest of Wiltshire and beyond. The family history is of interest in that two lines of the family continued in parallel for several generations, to be reunited in the 16th century. The two separate churches in West Dean became associated with the two sides of the family when the lands were divided between the descendants of Albreda and Isabel[3].

Fig. VI *Recently cut hazel coppice.(AB)*

Fig. VII *An old oak pollard near Queenwood Farm, East Tytherley.(AB)*

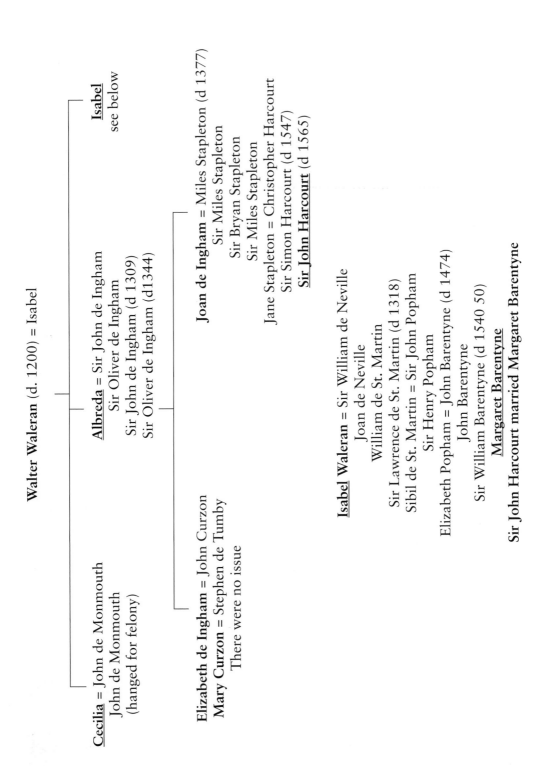

Walter Waleran (d. 1200) = Isabel

Cecilia = John de Monmouth
John de Monmouth
(hanged for felony)

Albreda = Sir John de Ingham
Sir Oliver de Ingham
Sir John de Ingham (d 1309)
Sir Oliver de Ingham (d1344)

Isabel
see below

Elizabeth de Ingham = John Curzon
Mary Curzon = Stephen de Tumby
There were no issue

Joan de Ingham = Miles Stapleton (d 1377)
Sir Miles Stapleton
Sir Bryan Stapleton
Sir Miles Stapleton
Jane Stapleton = Christopher Harcourt
Sir Simon Harcourt (d 1547)
Sir John Harcourt (d 1565)

Isabel Waleran = Sir William de Neville
Joan de Neville
William de St. Martin
Sir Lawrence de St. Martin (d 1318)
Sibil de St. Martin = Sir John Popham
Sir Henry Popham
Elizabeth Popham = John Barentyne (d 1474)
John Barentyne
Sir William Barentyne (d 1540 50)
Margaret Barentyne
Sir John Harcourt married Margaret Barentyne

Giffard

The Giffard family did not have a long association with the Dun Valley, but they owned the manors of both West Dean and East Tytherley during the latter part of the 16th century. **Anne**, wife of **Richard Giffard**, inherited the manor of East Tytherley fron Thomas Bainbridge, who was burnt at the stake in Winchester in 1559. Her son, **Henry Giffard**, died in 1592, leaving two sons, and the elder, William, succeeded his grandmother in 1594. He died in 1597 and the estate passed to his brother, Richard, who sold the manor estate to Henry Wallop in 1626. The remains of a very large monument to Richard Giffard, who died in 1568, and his wife, Anne, can still be seen today in East Tytherley church.

Henry Giffard bought West Dean manor in 1577 from the Harcourt family. On his death it passed to his son William and then to Richard, who sold the manor to John Evelyn.

Evelyn

George Evelyn (1526-1603) made his fortune from the manufacture of gunpowder, for which he was granted a monopoly, and the family continued to hold a patent for gunpowder production until the Civil Wars in 1642.

John Evelyn (1554-1627), George's son, inherited the chief mills in Kingston-upon-Hull, and managed the family's gunpowder production. He bought West Dean manor, which probably included the existing mansion house, although the house was considerably altered by succeeding generations.

↓

George Evelyn (1581-1636)

↓

Sir John Evelyn (1601-1685)

↓

Elizabeth Evelyn = **Robert Pierrepont** (1634-1690), Earl of Kingston-upon-Hull

↓

Evelyn Pierrepont (1665-1726) became the first Duke of Kingston in 1690 and Marquis of Dorchester in 1706

↓

Lady Mary Pierrepont (1689-1762) married Edward Wortley Montague, and became Lady Mary Wortley Montague.

Fig. VIII *The River Dun near East Dean.(AB)*

Fig. IX *Holbury Mill today.(AB)*

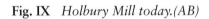

Fig. X *East Dean church, exterior and interior.(AB)*

Fig. 7 *West Dean House and the old church. (R. Colt Hoare)*

Fig. 8 *West Dean House, east front. (R.Colt Hoare)*

Robert Pierrepont was of ancient lineage, his family dating back to another Robert who held land in the reign of William II. Later generations of Pierreponts had married heiresses to land and fortunes, and Robert was the son and heir of Baron Pierrepont of Hanslope, Bucks. He would have been considered a very suitable husband for Elizabeth, the heiress to Sir John Evelyn.

Evelyn Pierrepont was succeeded by his grandson, Evelyn (1711-73) son of William, who had died in 1713. **Evelyn Pierrepont** died without issue in 1773[4].

West Dean House stood near the old church, overlooking a terraced garden with a park beyond. A large fishpond fed an ornamental canal, and the old motte on the top of the hill was converted into a bowling green. The house, which had stood empty for many years, was demolished when the estate was bought in 1819 by Charles Baring Wall, who owned Norman Court, but the surrounding buildings remained as the estate farm[5]. Inside the remains of the old church, now the Borbach Chantry Chapel (Fig.XI, p50), the elaborate memorials to the former lords of the manor have been preserved. The most impressive is the monument to John Evelyn (1554-1627) and his wife Elizabeth, which also features their eleven children in relief below the effigies of their parents (Fig.XII, p50). More restrained is the monument of John Evelyn (1601-1685) which is a life-sized marble bust. The memorial to Robert Pierrepont, the husband of Elizabeth Evelyn who inherited the manor, is a life-sized statue of the deceased, kneeling in prayer with an angel hovering above to support him. There is a lengthy epitaph on the doors of the monument (Figs.XIII, p50).

Lady Mary Wortley Montague, the daughter of Evelyn Pierrepont, spent part of her childhood at West Dean House with her grandmother, following the death of her mother. In 1699, her grandmother died and she went to live with her father at the family's Thoresby estate in Nottinghamshire. She was sent back to West Dean in 1712, when aged 23 and shortly before her marriage she had rejected the husband who had been chosen for her by her father. Soon afterwards Mary eloped with Edward Wortley Montague, and in 1716 they went to live in Turkey, where Edward had been appointed ambassador. Mary made the interesting observation while in Turkey that the local people were inoculating other inhabitants who had not had smallpox by scratching the skin with infected material, producing a relatively mild infection which promoted immunity to the disease. This was of considerable interest to Mary, who had been badly scarred by smallpox in 1715. When she returned to England, in spite of considerable medical opposition, she had her daughter inoculated by the method she had witnessed in Turkey, which was the first instance of smallpox vaccination in Britain. The disease was later controlled by the rather safer practice of inoculation with cowpox to produce immunity. Mary became a much-respected author of both poetry and prose, in addition to being a well known figure in contemporary society[6].

Fig. XI *The Borbach chapel, West Dean.(AB)*

Fig. XII *Memorial to John Evelyn.(AB)*   **Fig. XIII** *Memorial to Robert Pierrepont.(AB)*

Fig. XIV *Queenwood College. HRO ref. 6M76/G3*

John Evelyn (1620-1706), the celebrated diarist was also related to the Evelyns of West Dean, being the grandson of George (1526-1603) by his second wife. He was also the author of Silva, a discourse on trees and the propagation of timber, which he wrote in 1670, when improved methods of forestry were needed to increase timber production.

Whithed (Whitehead)

The manor of Norman Court which was situated in West Tytherley had close associations with the Dun Valley. Part of the parish of East Dean was held by the lord of Norman Court manor from 1486[7]. During the 19th century most of West Dean parish was acquired by successive owners of Norman Court; in 1820 the manor of West Dean was bought by Charles Baring Wall in 1820, and in 1868 Thomas Baring exchanged land which he held near Salisbury for Howe Farm, West Dean.

Norman Court, named after one of its early owners, Roger Norman, belonged to the Whithed, or Whitehead, family from the 1430s.

Sir Henry Whithed (d. 1629)
↓
Richard Whithed (1594-1663)

Richard inherited Norman Court when his father, Sir Henry Whithed, died in 1629. He was sheriff of Hampshire in 1636. During the Civil War he was a staunch Parliamentarian and a colonel of one of the Hampshire regiments. Richard saw very active service, and was present at attacks on Basing House and Bishop's Waltham palace.

↓
Francis Whithed
↓
Richard (son or brother of Francis)
↓
Henry Whithed married Mary, daughter of Richard Norton of Southwick

Their daughter, also called Mary, married **Alexander Thistlethwaite**, a member of the Thistlethwaite family of Winterslow, in 1717. In the 1750s **Robert Thistlethwaite** had the present Norman Court mansion house built on the hillside above the site of the old manor buildings.

Early in the 19th century Norman Court was bought by **Charles Wall**, who was succeeded by his son, **Charles Baring Wall**, in 1816. In 1853 the estate was inherited by Thomas Baring, the nephew of C. B. Wall's mother. **Thomas Baring**, an MP for Huntingdon, was head of the Baring Brothers bank, and had other estates in Hampshire[8].

Rolle

In 1654 Sir Francis Rolle of Shapwick, Somerset, purchased the manors of East Tytherley and Lockerley. Unfortunately he was a supporter of the Duke of Monmouth, the illegitimate son of Charles II who raised a rebellion against James II in 1685, which culminated in defeat at the battle of Sedgemoor. Sir Francis was executed in the Tower of London and was buried in East Tytherley in 1686. As a result of her marriage settlement his widow, Dame Priscilla, inherited the manors.

Dame Priscilla died in 1708, and the estate passed to her grandson John Rolle, whose father had predeceased Dame Priscilla. Sarah Rolle, who founded the school in East Tytherley (see chap.10) was the daughter of Sir Francis and Dame Priscilla. John shot himself in the grand saloon of Tytherley manor house in 1726, and after this unfortunate incident his brother Samuel inherited the estate. Samuel Rolle died of 'gout in his stomach' in 1729, leaving his estates in Hampshire and Somerset to Colonel John Rolle. Colonel John died in 1730 and the estate passed to his second son John.

In 1755, under the terms of a settlement made by Col. John Rolle in 1729, the Hampshire and Somerset estates passed from John, who had now inherited an estate in Oxfordshire, to Denys Rolle (1748-97), his younger brother. Denys already had a substantial estate in Devon, but he made East Tytherley manor his main residence and it was Denys who planted the cedar trees in the park land around the manor house, some of which are still there today.

In 1801 Denys Rolle's son, Lord John Rolle, sold the manors of East Tytherley and Lockerley to William Steele Wakeford of Andover, a draper and proprietor of Andover Old Bank. Wakeford died in 1819, and it is not certain that he ever lived in East Tytherley. A few years later in 1822 his sons, whose banking business was on the verge of collapse, sold the estate[9].

Fig. XV *16th century room with the central hearth and unglazed windows.(AB)*

Fig. XVI *17th century fireplace with a chimney.(AB)*

Fig. XVII *Early 17th century house exterior, with unglazed windows.(AB)*

Fig. XVIII *Tudor bedroom with tester bed and truckle bed below.(AB)*

Goldsmid/Bailey

In about 1822 the East Tytherley estate was sold to Francis Bailey and Isaac Goldsmid. Goldsmid wanted to buy a landed manorial estate, but he was a Jew and under the law as it stood at that time Jews were precluded from holding land in Britain. He therefore bought the East Tytherley and Lockerley manors in conjunction with Francis Bailey. When the Emancipation Act was passed, which allowed Goldsmid to own the estate, Bailey refused to give up the property. A compromise was reached and in 1833 the ownership of the estate was divided into two parts, giving Goldsmid the manor house and manorial rights and half the land. Bailey's part was sold in 1849 and bought by Sir William Cooke, who built himself a house which he named Oaklands.

Dalgety

Frederick Gonnerman Dalgety made his fortune by providing supplies to sheep farmers in Australia, and shipping their wool to England. He had sailed out there as a boy of 16 years of age in 1833. He returned to England in 1854, married a year later and had 13 children. In 1866 he bought Sir William Cooke's part of the East Tytherley and Lockerley estate, and proceeded to pull down Oaklands, replacing it with Lockerley Hall on the same site. In 1879 he purchased the other half of the estate from the Goldsmid family, thus returning the estate to its original size. However, there were now two mansion houses. The Dalgetys continued to occupy Lockerley Hall, while the old manor house, which had stood unoccupied except for caretakers since 1854, became increasingly derelict[10,11].

Sandys

William, Lord Sandys was granted the priory site and manor estate of Mottisfont following the dissolution of the monasteries in 1536. Sandys was the chamberlain of Henry VIII and having acquired the priory for an annual rent of £51, he set about turning it into a country residence. The old priory buildings were modified and added to rather than completely demolished, a process which continued with later generations, so that parts of the priory are still visible today.

5
Religion, Ideology and Idealism

Religious belief and the church as an institution both played a huge part in the lives of people from all sections of society, not only in medieval times but also throughout the following centuries. The Church was a powerful force, relatively independent of the Crown and State, which affected daily life in all communities. People were baptized, married and buried by the Church, they paid a proportion of their hard-won income to support and maintain it, and the church courts dealt with such matters as failure to observe Holy Days, and disputes over wills and testaments.

Before the 19th century most of the population in rural communities was illiterate, and the religious teaching by the Church, reinforced by the colourful pictures on the church walls depicting biblical events and religious themes, would have had a profound effect which it is hard to imagine today. The Church set standards of behaviour, aided by threats of eternal damnation of the souls of the wicked, while giving comfort and hope to the large sections of society who struggled with poverty, and to the many suffering from pain, disability and disease. The Church also had practical effects on daily life and the strict observance of the Sabbath ensured that the workforce rested on one day a week, even when it was vital that the corn was harvested, or the hay made before the weather broke. The only holidays which most of society ever had were the Holy Days, and the celebration of the major religious festivals, such as Christmas, added the only colour to what for many people must have been very drab lives. The Catholic religion fulfilled more than just the spiritual requirements of rural, largely illiterate communities. Catholicism was a highly visual experience and the churches were richly decorated with images and pictures which were readily understood. The Crucifix, set on a rood beam or screen between the nave and the chancel, usually had a doom painting above or behind it showing the Last Judgement in graphic detail, and the plastered church walls were covered with paintings showing scenes from the gospels[1]. The burning of candles at side altars, the telling of the rosary beads and just watching the priest in his elaborate vestments were all visual experiences which must have had considerable impact on the local population.

Processions were a major feature of the liturgy, Sunday Mass was preceded by a procession and all the most important feasts were marked by processions in which everyone took part. At Rogationtide a procession 'beat the bounds' of the parish, which had the practical value of establishing the boundary when there were no maps, and the local villagers could not have read them if there had been. A young boy was beaten at each boundary point, which ensured that the next generation never forgot precisely where the boundaries lay.

The religious centre of the village was the parish church, and its importance ensured that it was a substantial, and often very imposing, building, when compared with the houses of the parishioners; only the lord of the manor was likely to have a bigger building. Saxon churches had often been wooden structures, but following the Norman Conquest almost all the pre-existing churches were reconstructed, and many new ones were built on the manor estates of the new Norman lords. Stone, being the most enduring building material, was used where it was readily available, but in other areas far from a stone quarry, stone blocks were often used to support the corners of otherwise rubble walls. The early Norman churches were usually fairly simple in plan, the simplest form being just a nave and sanctuary, which was either square-ended or apsidal. Throughout the medieval period churches were founded, rebuilt or enlarged by individual patrons, such as the local lord of the manor.

The Dun Valley is a considerable distance from stone quarries but there are abundant quantities of chalk and flint, and the local Norman church builders made good use of them. Thick substantial walls were constructed from chalk, rubble and flints, supported at the corners by stone quoins, and plastered over to make them weatherproof. In later centuries bricks were often used for enlargements to the original building, and knapped flints provided a durable exterior surface. Nothing remains of the original Saxon churches in the local villages, and their Norman replacements are hard to decipher as they have been extensively rebuilt during the succeeding centuries. In three cases, East Grimstead, West Dean and Lockerley, they were totally replaced in the 19th century.

The parish churches

Both the original St. Mary's in West Dean and the chapel in East Grimstead were replaced in the 19th century, but fortunately G.S. Master, rector of West Dean, writing in 1885 gives a contemporary description of the old churches, which had been demolished some twenty years earlier[2]. St. Mary's

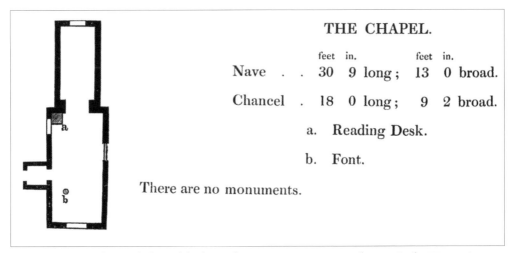

THE CHAPEL.

	feet	in.		feet	in.
Nave . .	30	9	long;	13	0 broad.
Chancel .	18	0	long;	9	2 broad.

a. Reading Desk.

b. Font.

There are no monuments.

Fig. 9 *Plan of the old chapel at East Grimstead. (R.Colt Hoare)*

had rubble, chalk, flint and sandstone walls, which were plastered over externally, and there was a wooden turret. The ground-plan was a chancel and nave, with a chantry (see below) and a south porch. East Grimstead he describes as a 'poor building of chalk without any feature of interest'. However, it is of interest historically in that it had remained a very simple building with just a nave and square-ended chancel, with a porch as the only addition. Colt Hoare in 1837 provides a ground plan and states that there were no monuments (Fig. 9). It had always been a chapel annexed to West Dean.

East Tytherley, East Dean and Lockerley were all chapelries attached to the church of Mottisfont in 1086, and both East Dean and Lockerley continued to be so until the 19th century. St. Winfrid's church, East Dean, still shows much of its early form although there are inevitably many later renovations; the nave has been lengthened and the chancel arch widened and there is also an interesting 18th century gallery. Much of the original appearance is retained as the walls are still mainly rubble and flint rendered over, and supported by blocks of iron-stone at the corners. There is a small bell tower at the west end. If it were possible to go back in time and compare the church as it would have been in Norman times with the present church, the most noticeable difference would be the amount of light inside, as most of the windows have been considerably enlarged. The 14-15th century door is a particularly well-preserved medieval feature (Fig.X, p47).

The church of St. John in Lockerley was demolished and replaced in 1889.

The old church was thought to have been built by William Briwere, the founder of Mottisfont Priory, c 1200, and Fig. 12 shows what it looked like before it was pulled down. Like the other churches it had originally been a very simple structure, with a nave and chancel, entered by a south porch. St. Peter's church in East Tytherley has been extensively renovated, but was not completely replaced during the enthusiastic church-building Victorian era. The walls were raised, the roof replaced, a transept added on the south side and a new bell tower added. However, parts of the walls are from the original structure, and the position of the building in relation to the old manor site can be clearly seen (Fig.II, p8). The church had an 18th century gallery, now removed, similar to East Dean, and a large box pew for the lord of the manor and his family.

In the early Middle Ages no seating was provided in the nave of a church, except for an occasional stone bench around the side, and in a small village church with no stone structures there was probably no seating at all. Later on wooden benches and pews were added, and by the 15th century the local lord of the manor had a boxed-in private pew[3]. G.S. Master describes a large wainscoted pew with Jacobean carvings for the lord of West Dean manor in St. Mary's[4]. The appearance of the interior of churches in medieval times would have been very different from that of today as the plaster on the walls was covered with brightly painted pictures and patterns. Any parts of the walls where the plaster was not decorated were whitewashed, since the fashion for exposing and displaying stones and brickwork in the interior of buildings is relatively recent.

The person around whom the religious life in the parish revolved was, of course, the local priest. The parish was the community which supported the parish priest, and he was responsible for the spiritual well-being of his parishioners. The tithes which were collected by the priest represented a tenth of the produce of the parish lands, in money or in kind. It was originally intended that one quarter of the tithes should go to the bishop if he required it, one quarter to the priest, one quarter to the poor and one to the repair of the church fabric. This was not maintained and it was later accepted that the rector, or the administrator who held the tithes of the parish, should be responsible for the fabric of the chancel, and the parishioners would be responsible for the rest[5]. Tithes were payable on corn, hay, wood, fruit and other crops, as well as on animal products such as lambs, calves, wool, milk, eggs and honey. They were payable to the rector of the parish, who might be the resident priest, or the living might be held by a bishop, monastic house or college. Where there was an absentee rector he usually appointed a vicar to carry out his parish duties, and the vicar received some of the tithes. The 'great tithes', the tithes on grain, hay and wood which were the most valuable, went to the rector, and the rest, or 'small tithes', went to the vicar. Following the dissolution of the monasteries in the 1530s, their tithes went to the Crown, which then sold them to laymen[6].

Although the tithes were originally paid in kind, they gradually became monetary payments in many parishes. However, payment in kind was not replaced entirely until the Tithe Commutation Act of 1836. In order to commute the tithes into a tithe rent-charge, and to settle any dispute between the parishioners and the tithe-holders, the land and its productivity had to be surveyed. As part of this procedure a detailed tithe map of the parish was produced, and these maps are an invaluable source of information in the study of the local history of a rural area.

In addition to the receipt of tithes, the incumbent of the parish church had an area of land in the parish, the glebe, to support himself. Just as other land holders had their land in scattered strips spread across the open arable fields, so too did the parish priest, and his animals grazed in the common flocks and herds alongside those of the other villagers.

East Tytherley Glebe Terrier (record of land held) 1639[7]

The terrier of the glebe lands belonging to the Parsonadge of East Tytherley 1639.

In primis one parsonadge house with one barne, one stable, backside, gardens and orchard, 3 acres of meadow, 12 acres of coppice wood, 60 acres of down for sheepe, 60 acres of arable land, 18 acres of pasture.

One house and garden called the Vicaridge house, one tenement built upon one parcell of land called the Vicaridge Meadow

Christopher Cosier curat ibid (curate)

Augustine Blake, Thomas Downes – church wardens

The priest also had a substantial residence, the rectory or vicarage according to his status, and it is possible to get some idea of what the later houses were like from the glebe terriers as above. The glebe terrier for East Dean (1690-1760) lists *'a vicarage house containing four ground rooms with two garrets, a garden plot of half an acre adjoining'*[8]. The rectory in West Dean at a comparable date was a fine building. G. S. Master describes it as it appeared in the 19th century, when it had obviously had some additions to the original building, as 'a commodious edifice of brick, standing in a pleasant lawn and backed by fine elm trees'. There was a range of excellent stables and outbuildings and a fine walled kitchen garden, an acre in extent[9]. This house still stands on Rectory Hill in West Dean today. There are no records of earlier buildings, but the priest was always likely to have had a relatively large dwelling when compared with the other village houses of the time.

It is also possible to get some idea of the domestic lifestyle of the village priest from the probate inventories of Tudor and Stuart times. Robert Wheatley, cleric of East Dean, who died in 1637, occupied a substantial, but not palatial, house with a hall, buttery and two upper chambers. He had a yard behind with a stable for his horse, a garden and had two acres of corn in the common field[10].

All Saints, West Dean

The interrelationship between the churches in the Dun Valley has already been referred to; East Tytherley, Lockerley and East Dean were chapels annexed to Mottisfont, which was held by York cathedral, and East Grimstead was a chapelry of West Dean church. Originally there was another church in the valley, All Saints in West Dean, which stood on the south side of the river. All Saints was in the diocese of Winchester, whereas St. Mary's, West Dean was in Salisbury diocese, and there were two distinct parishes, each with its own rector. In 1473 a decision was made to unite the two churches, since the number of parishioners attached to All Saints, and the value of their tithes, had diminished to the point at which it was no longer viable. The living was vacant and could not be filled, and the church fabric needed some attention. All Saints duly became a chapel dependent on the church of St. Mary. The former parishioners were to pay their tithes to the rector of St. Mary's, who was then to pay 20d to the bishop of Winchester at Easter, 8d to the prior and convent of Winchester, and 8d to the archdeacon. All Saints would continue to be used for services, as the rector of St. Mary's was to celebrate mass there once a week. The poor state of repair of the church needed to be addressed and the chancel particularly required considerable renovation. The maintenance of the chancel had been specified as one of the responsibilities of the rector of St. Mary's when he took over the church, but he was unlikely to have been very enthusiastic about expensive renovation work on a church with few parishioners. The deteriorating state of the church fabric was probably a major factor which led to the ultimate demise of All Saints, and at an unknown date it was finally demolished. The precise whereabouts then seem to have been forgotten, until a stone coffin was dug up in 1870 in a field; the field, not surprisingly, was called Allhallon[11].

The two separate churches in West Dean were closely connected to the two separate branches of the Walerand family; the descendants of Albreda, including Oliver de Ingham, held the advowson of St. Mary's, whereas Isabel's descendants held that of All Saints (see chap. 4). This became an issue when the churches were united under one rector, but the arrangement that the two families should alternate in their right to choose the rector whenever the position became vacant was rendered unnecessary when the families were re-united by marriage in the 16th century.

The chantry chapel, West Dean

In St. Mary's there was a chantry chapel founded in 1333 by Robert de Borbach, and it can still be seen today, as it was left standing when the church was demolished. It was renovated to become the mortuary chapel and stands in the old graveyard (Fig.XI, p50).

The relationship between the living and the dead was an important part of the late medieval religion. The souls of the departed who were destined for Heaven had to spend time in purgatory, where they received punishment for their sins before they were admitted into Heaven. The Church taught that the prayers of the living could help the souls who were in purgatory, and altars and chantry chapels, where masses could be said for the departed, became a common feature in even modest-sized churches[12].

Chantries first became popular in the late 13th century. When a person died a mass was said for his soul by the parish priest, and money was often left by the wealthy to have masses said periodically for an agreed time afterwards and for an obit, the term for the celebration of mass each year on the anniversary of the death. During the 14th century chantries were an important part of the religious life of the wealthy, and endowments of lands, rents and houses were left to provide a stipend for a priest to say masses for the founder at a specified altar in a church, or in a special chantry chapel. Money was usually also left as part of the endowment to provide for the local poor and needy. The endowment of a perpetual chantry chapel, which included an altar and the tomb of the founder, was costly, and therefore only for the very wealthy. It also had to be sufficient to provide the stipend for a priest to say mass daily, and money to maintain the chantry fabric. Other, more minor, provisions included the cost of candles to be burnt at the altar. In order to ensure that the chantry priest occupied his time in a useful and not unseemly way in between his not very onerous duties, he was usually given other tasks, such as helping the parish priest, and sometimes there were instructions about his conduct; for example, he was not to play dice or frequent the local ale-house. Not surprisingly, the number of foundations increased rapidly after the Black Death, when the fear and uncertainty of daily life turned people's thoughts to their own mortality[13].

Robert de Borbach endowed his chantry chapel in St. Mary's with the collection of rents to the value of 100s a year from tenements in East Grimstead. The appointed chaplain was to say mass daily in the chantry for the souls of the late king, Edward I, the Earl of Gloucester and Hertford and his wife, John de Ingham and his wife, for the good estate while living of the Bishop of Salisbury, Oliver de Ingham, Robert le Boor and himself, and for their souls when they had departed. De Borbach provided suitable vestments and furnishings for the chapel, including a chalice, a missal, a washing basin and ewer and a five gallon jar[14]. He little knew that within a few years the whole village would be devastated by the Black Death.

Death, and the salvation of their souls, was an important aspect of life for the rich and powerful in the Middle Ages. It became less so in later centuries, but the wealthy still provided for the erection of elaborate memorials and tombs to ensure that they were remembered in this world, and that their families continued to be honoured. Even in small parish churches there were elaborate monuments, and the beautiful memorial to Sir John Evelyn in the mortuary chapel in West Dean, and the remains of the memorial to Richard Giffard (1568) in East Tytherley church demonstrate how strong the tradition was.

Monasteries

From the Norman Conquest onwards the wealthy paid heavily in order to ensure the eternal salvation of their souls with grants of land, money and rents to the church, and by founding new churches on their estates or providing extensions to older, established ones. The monasteries also benefitted from their gifts and many became rich and powerful as a consequence.

Monasticism in the form which became familiar throughout the Middle Ages began with St. Benedict in the 6th century. However, the monastic movement was preceded by hermits, either solitary or in small bands, who removed themselves from the world to live a life of contemplation and prayer. At a later time similar small groups which had been sent out as cells from existing monasteries to exploit a distant estate, lived in seclusion in isolated places, and they received some degree of official protection and support[15]. It was likely to have been one such cell that in 1334 was granted:

'Protection for a year to Brother John de Warrewyk, a hermit dwelling in Bentley Wood, by Claryndon, co. Wilts, and his men, seeking alms. And letters are directed to all bailiffs and others to protect them'[16].

An area within Bentley Wood is still called Armitage, or Hermitage, coppice today, and was probably the site where they had their dwelling.

The foundation of the Benedictine monasteries in Saxon times established the tradition of monastic houses, where the monks divided their time between prayer, reading the bible, meditation and manual work. They were bound under the rule of their order to lead a life of poverty, chastity and obedience. These ideals tended to have been forgotten as monasteries became rich and powerful, and as a consequence other orders, such as the reformed Benedictines from the abbey of Cluny in Burgundy and the Cistercians, were founded with the intention of returning to a stricter and more ascetic lifestyle. In addition to the monastic orders there were also the Augustinian canons, who lived together in monastic-like communities under similar rules, but who were able to act as priests in local churches. The Augustinians, or Black Canons as they were called after the colour of their habits, first came to England in the early 12th century and established about two hundred modest-sized monastic houses around the country.

Two of these are of interest in connection with the Dun Valley, Mottisfont priory and the priory of St. Denys near Southampton, both of which had land and influence in the local parishes.

The monasteries in general owned large tracts of land, and in downland areas had many thousands of sheep in their sheep flocks. They were a major landowning force in the country until the dissolution of the monasteries in the 1530s. Initially the religious houses managed their landed estates directly, or in demesne, but in the late 14th and early 15th centuries they turned to leasing the land out and receiving the income instead.

Mottisfont priory was founded by William Briwere, who held the manors of King's Somborne and Stockbridge, and Briwere's original endowments were later added to by his son William, who donated the church of King's Somborne, a mill and land in Stockbridge and rents in Mottisfont and elsewhere, in return for a mass to be celebrated in the priory on his anniversary each year. Other endowments ensured that they became a viable, and wealthy, institution, and the priory acquired eleven manor estates around the local countryside, which they managed partly in demesne but also leased out some of the land. One of their manors was in East Dean parish, and a survey carried out in 1340-42 showed that 68 acres of arable land and 7 ½ acres of meadow were managed in demesne, and that there was pasture in common for 160 sheep. There were also 199 acres of arable and 4 ½ acres of meadow which were leased out[17].

The other priory that had land in the Dun Valley was St. Denys priory, a small Augustinian priory at Portswood, near Southampton, which was founded in the 12th century. In the early 13th century a number of rural families around East Tytherley who were looking for spiritual support made endowments to the priory so that they could have masses celebrated for their souls, particularly on anniversaries. The Columbars, who were lords of the manor of East Tytherley in the late 12th and early 13th centuries, made several substantial endowments to the priory. Documents in the cartulary of St. Denys priory show that sometime in the late 12th or early 13th centuries Michael (or grandson Michael, there is some doubt) Columbar granted all the tithes of his assarts and newly broken land; these would have been areas of woodland and rough grazing which had been recently cleared and converted into arable and pasture[18]. Michael Columbar had already given to the priory the church of East Tytherley, as well as land, common rights of pasture and some tithes, which was confirmed by his son Gilbert in the

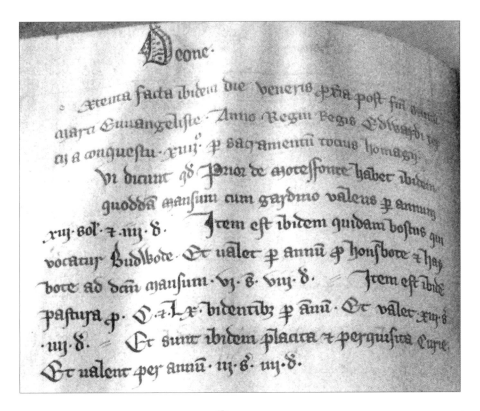

Dean

Survey made there Friday first after the feast of Saint Mark Evangelist in the 14th year of the reign of Edward III after the conquest on the oath of the homage.

Six say that the Prior of Mottisfont has a mansion there with a garden, value per annum 13s 4d. Also there is a wood called Budwood. And it is worth per annum for housebote and haybote to the mansion 6s 8d. Likewise there is pasture for 160 sheep per annum. And it is worth 13s 4d. And there are the pleas and perquisites of the court there. And they are worth 3s 4d per annum.

Housebote - wood for house building and repairs.

Haybote - wood for fencing.

Fig. 10 *Mottisfont Priory rental, 1340. HRO ref. 13M63/3 (AB)*

early 13th century[19]. Also around that time Thomas Columbar granted to the priory a moiety of Basset Mill, which stood on the later Lockerley Mill site, although he did retain part of the multure (payments paid by the manor tenants to have their corn ground there), and he also gave some land in Lockerley[20].

Other local benefactors who added to the holdings of the priory in East Tytherley and Lockerley were Walter Basset, who donated his half of Basset Mill and a small area of land around it[21], and Robert de Auuiler, who gave the priory an estate in Lockerley, which included the right to take wood for constructing and repairing houses and fences, and common grazing rights for cattle, sheep, goats and pigs[22]. The priory of St. Denys thus became a major institution within the parishes of East Tytherley and Lockerley. The Prior and his canons controlled the church in East Tytherley and would have taken most of the tithes of that parish, and although there is no evidence that the canons actually served as priests in the churches which came into their possession, they appear to have had a cell in East Tytherley and to have built a house there, which was referred to in 1227 as the Prior's house[23]. There was also a court of canons there.

The 16th century saw great changes in the religious life of England. During the 1530s, Henry VIII, after an unsuccessful battle to have his marriage to Catherine of Aragon annulled, finally seized spiritual authority from the Pope and declared himself Supreme Head of the church in England. Henry VIII had a desperate need to raise money, mainly because he was fighting the French. Imposing taxation was always very unpopular and liable to cause rebellion, so the dissolution of the monasteries and the expropriation of all the monastic lands by the Crown, which brought huge sums of money and vast areas of land into the royal coffers, was an easier and more lucrative option. Henry also debased the coinage in order to raise more money, but most of what he had gained was spent on war with France. By the end of Henry's reign much of the newly-acquired monastic property had been sold to wealthy subjects in order to raise yet more money[24].

Although significant amounts of land in the Dun Valley were owned by the priories of Mottisfont and St. Denys, the villagers may not have felt the change too acutely when the estates were sold. The land had been increasingly managed by laymen who rented the land, so that the management may not have been drastically different. By the 16th century the monasteries had accumulated such extensive endowments of land, property and tithes that they had become very wealthy. They had let out their estates on long leases rather than managing them directly, collecting the rents and living in a relatively luxurious manner, far removed from the ascetic ideals of bygone ages. One change which people would have felt was a marked rise in rents, but this was mainly due to the debasement of the coinage, which caused soaring prices so that landlords everywhere had to raise their rents whenever they had the opportunity.

Henry's break with Rome began the move away from Catholicism, which was continued by his successors, except for Queen Mary, who reinstated the Latin mass and tried to reverse the changes. Queen Elizabeth, and the Stuart kings who succeeded her, tried to follow a more moderate course by developing Anglicanism with an English prayer book and the bible translated into English, but without moving too far towards the Puritan movement, which was gathering momentum. The Puritans maintained that a believer could establish contact with God without the intervention of the Church and priests, and that all remnants of the Catholic ritual in church services should be abolished[25]. All these changes must have created considerable upheaval in the parish churches, and alienated the minority who held strong beliefs at both ends of the spectrum. On the one hand there were those who clung to the Catholic traditions, even though there were heavy fines for failure to attend the parish church. These 'recusants' were a relatively small band of prosperous Catholics who could afford to pay the fines imposed, and the Catholics were the first section of the community to break away from the parish church as a social unit. At the opposite end of the spectrum the Puritans caused far greater disruption in their determination to root out the last vestiges of the old form of religion in Britain, with all its visual and ceremonial aspects. During the early part of the 17th century the Puritans tried to reform the Church from within, putting great emphasis on sermons preached from the pulpit, rather than participation in the service by the congregation, and tried to establish Sunday as a day of prayer, without the traditional communal sports and activities after the service was over[26]. Divisions within the church steadily deteriorated and were a major factor in causing civil war in England during the 1640s.

The Civil War

There were many contributing factors which led England into civil war in 1642. The monarchy had had a long-term financial struggle to raise money since the time of Henry VIII, and successive monarchs had sold off property and land, and had tried to impose taxes on the general population. In 1639-40 Charles I tried to raise money to pay for the fleet, when he was fighting the French and Spaniards and attempts to collect 'ship money' were very unpopular. He also tried to secure financial aid through Parliament to suppress the Presbyterian risings in Scotland; Charles had tried to impose the Book of Common Prayer on the Scottish Church, and met with total opposition. In England there were deep divisions about the form which Christianity should adopt, and as open warfare became inevitable, the country as a whole was very divided over which side should be taken. Many Parliamentarians, opposing the king because they were critical of political issues, became allied with the Puritan Movement.

Some counties were united in their support for either the king or parliament, but many others were divided among themselves. Locally Richard Whitehead, of Norman Court, West Tytherley, and a shire Member of Parliament, was a Parliamentarian, as were Sir John Evelyn, of West Dean, and Francis St. Barbe of Broadlands, Romsey. On the Royalist side were the Sandys family of Mottisfont, who had acquired the old priory and its lands, and Lord John Paulet, Marquis of Winchester. In the early part of the war both sides relied on local county families to take the lead in forming an army. The main source of soldiers was the trained military bands of local villagers, a home defence system which had not been called into action as no warfare had taken place on English soil for many centuries. They provided their own arms, and were supposed to attend muster during the summer months for training (see chap 6). Richard Whitehead raised an early regiment, assembling 300 men for the Parliamentarian army in 1642[27]. In Wiltshire Sir John Evelyn was actively engaged on the same side, and from 1644 West Dean House acted as one of the Parliamentary garrisons. Both sides fortified towns and churches to form major garrisons, and also created smaller ones in rural manor houses, which could maintain control over the local countryside.

In 1644 most of the country south-west of Oxford was in Royalist hands, and the Parliamentarians tried to establish a hold in the eastern part of the area by taking a few strategic positions so that they could gradually move westwards. Longford Castle, south of Salisbury was held by the Royalists, and when Major Wansey with three troops of Parliamentary horse soldiers, arrived there, he found it formidably defended, so he placed a garrison in Sir John Evelyn's house in West Dean. From there he could keep both Longford Castle and the city of Salisbury, which had not yet fallen to the Royalists, under observation. In November 1644 the Royalists moved into Salisbury, and after some skirmishes fortified the Cathedral Close. A few weeks later Col. Edmund Ludlow attacked the Close and fortified the

Fig. 11 *Cavalier soldiers. (Hablot Browne)*

detached belfry which at that time stood in the Cathedral Close. However, the Royalists won the battle and Ludlow retreated to Southampton. West Dean was then left as the only remaining Parliamentary stronghold in the area, and it was evacuated shortly afterwards[28].

The Royalist base in Salisbury did not last long and they left the town a few months later. In 1645 the Parliamentarian New Model Army was formed under the command of Sir Thomas Fairfax, and at about the same time Parliamentary troops under Waller and Cromwell moved westwards, to start attacking the Royalist-held regions in earnest[29]. Warfare continued on and off until 1649, when Charles I was tried and beheaded. His son, Charles, continued the fight but was defeated and had to retreat abroad, leaving Parliament in power under Oliver Cromwell, who became Lord Protector of the Commonwealth.

Life in the countryside in and around the Dun Valley during the Civil War must have been an anxious and difficult time. The armies of both sides caused much general disruption in the country as a whole, and locally when there were troops in West Dean they no doubt behaved in much the same way. Horses were often commandeered or stolen by passing soldiers, and farm work was disrupted by demands for labourers and carts to transport goods or to build fortifications. The armies also demanded supplies to feed the troops and their horses. The cannon balls found at East Dean Manor, which can be seen today displayed inside East Dean church, are a notable reminder that troops moving around the area would not have been an enjoyable experience for the local villagers.

The Restoration and afterwards

In 1660 the monarchy was restored and Charles II became king. Warfare was over and a monarchy had been created which was answerable to Parliament to a greater extent than previously. The countryside had gradually returned to normal, but religious life had changed. Christianity remained permanently divided, and the parish churches no longer represented all sections of their local communities. Under the general term of Dissenters or Nonconformists there were Presbyterians, Congregationalists and Baptists, who were gradually allowed more freedom to separate from the Church of England. In 1689 the Toleration Act officially recognised the Protestant Dissenters, but the country as a whole remained wary of Catholicism, and while allowing its existence, limited the offices which could be held by Catholics. From 1689 onwards the Church of England no longer had an official monopoly on Christian worship in Britain, and people could choose whether they went to church or to a meeting house. However, in spite of the new enthusiasm for different forms of worship, the rural parish churches survived and flourished.

Church fittings had been subject to many changes between the Reformation in the 1530s and the Restoration in 1660. The bitter conflicts over what were the essentials of religion, and what form services should take, had led to the furnishings being confiscated, changed and ripped out on numerous occasions, only to be replaced again at a later date. The churches as they emerged from the Civil War gradually developed into their modern form. Altar rails, which had been a source of much dispute, became universal, the altar within was often raised, and the table covered with an elaborate cloth; the table with seats placed down the centre of the chancel, favoured by the Puritans, had been eliminated permanently. Chantry chapels had gone, but the elaborate memorials to commemorate the lives of the local gentry flourished, and can still be seen today decorating our local churches.

Some idea of the state of the Dun Valley churches in the 18th century can be gained from the replies of the curates of the Hampshire churches to the bishop's visitations of 1725 and 1765[30].

Visitation of 1725. East Tytherley.

Thomas Mundy – curate
Area   1500 acres
Population   156
Marriages 1,   Births 7,   Burials 5
Patrons   John Rolle esq
Chapels   none
Lecturers   'I am at present the curate'
Papists   none
Dissenters   none
Gentry   John Rolle esq
Schools   1 charity school founded by Sarah Rolle, spinster. The school is unendowed. 40 scholars. The master is Peter Barber.
Charities   no charities have been given to the parish and no hospitals
Post-town   Andover

Visitation of 1765. East Dean

Edward Jones – rector (Edward Jones was rector of Mottisfont. He took services during the week).
John Evans – curate
Repair   yes the chapel has lately been put into good order
Services   once a day only
Sacrament   yes
Registers   yes
Terrier   Don't know
Churchyard   yes;no
Alterations   no
Impropriation   the stipend paid me for Sunday duty of the chapel £30 per annum

Residence
Dissenters   no
Loss of benefaction   no
Misbehaviour   no; yes (?)

There seems to have been some doubt about the level of improper behaviour in the local community. The curate in 1765 came out from a school in Romsey to serve East Dean and Lockerley churches.

Visitation of 1765. Lockerley

John Evans – curate (he took the service on Sundays) *the gentleman resident at Mottesfont does the weekly duty*

Dissenters   some few Anabaptists have built a room to assemble in

The Nonconformist movement did not affect the support which the gentry gave to the established church, and during the 18th century the lord of the manor figured prominently in the rural parish church. He maintained his historic right to select the parson, who therefore owed his position to the lord and in return helped to maintain the village social order. Most of the congregation were tenant farmers and estate workers, and the church wardens were usually the local yeoman farmers. The estate hierarchy was reflected in the organisation of the church, even determining which pews people sat in, but for good or ill it did provide social stability.

19th century changes

The 19th century was a time of great changes in the outward expression of the Anglican religion throughout the country. During the Victorian era many of the old parish churches were extensively renovated, enlarged, rebuilt and not infrequently demolished and replaced. In England as a whole about 7000 churches were restored. The main instigators were the wealthy estate owners who, having expanded and 'modernised' their houses, started work on the local church. Of the churches in the Dun Valley, West Dean, East Grimstead and Lockerley were all totally replaced, while St. Peter's in East Tytherley underwent considerable renovation. Only St. Winfrid's in East Dean remained essentially unaltered. The mood of the age was to build for the future, the Victorians were not interested in conserving the past, and most of their buildings were large and grandiose, reflecting the prosperity of the industrial nation and the status and wealth of the expanding empire. Interestingly their new village churches were built very much on the pattern developed over previous centuries, constructed in traditional shapes with traditional fittings. Gothic architecture was particularly popular with the Victorians, especially the Decorated period.

In West Dean the new church of St. Mary's was built on a fresh site further down the hill than the old church. It was erected in 1868, with money provided by Thomas Baring, of Norman Court, who was also lord of the

Fig. 12 *The old church at Lockerley c1880. HRO ref.65M89/Z151/2 (AB)*

Fig. 13 *Lockerley church today.(AB)*

manor of West Dean, and is essentially Early English in character. The old chapel in East Grimstead had already been replaced in 1856, with the new building being erected on the same site as the old one. It was funded by the family of the patron and former rector of the parish, the Rev. Henry Glossop, and is described by G.S. Master as 'a little gem of the first pointed style'[31].

The new church in Lockerley was built in 1889 by F.G. Dalgety, who had bought the manors of East Tytherley and Lockerley in 1879. The church in East Tytherley had already been extensively renovated, and when Dalgety had built Lockerley Hall he put his energy and money into providing a new church in Lockerley. The mood was again to keep to a traditional form, and the church was built in the 15th century style (Fig. 13).

The estate of East Tytherley was divided for a period during the 19th century and the owners of both parts used their money and enthusiasm to make changes to the church of St. Peter's. William Fothergill Cooke, one of the inventors of the electric telegraph, purchased half the estate in 1849, which did not include the manor house. He therefore built a new house, Oaklands, on the site where Lockerley Hall now stands. In 1852 he then made several alterations and improvements to the church, adding a south transept, and a porch to the north door. The other half of the estate belonged to Isaac Goldsmid, followed by his son, Sir Francis Goldsmid, who funded a major restoration of the church in 1862. Sir Francis also built a new parsonage to the north of the church in 1858. The Dalgetys later owned both parts of the estate, and the Dalgety tomb is in the East Tytherley churchyard.

St. Winfrid's church in East Dean retains much of its original form and is unusual in not having been dramatically changed during the 19th century. The church was annexed to Mottisfont church until 1884, together with Lockerley, after which it became a chapelry attached to Lockerley. East Dean parish and village were divided between the distant manors of Norman Court, West Tytherley, and Mottisfont, and therefore there was no resident lord of the manor with the enthusiasm for total change. Consequently the 19th century improvements were more modest, and simply continued the general updating and renovation which had taken place over many generations. The west gable-end had been rebuilt and has a circular 18th century window, and there is an 18th century gallery covering what is assumed to be an earlier extension to the church. There were renovations carried out in 1895, and at that time the opening between the chancel and the nave was enlarged (Fig.X, p47).

The income of the parish incumbent in the 18th century was very variable, and was sometimes rather inadequate even when the tithes and the glebe land were taken into account, and this led to some of them holding more than one living. Poorly paid curates were then often employed to take services in the more distant churches. This became common within the Winchester diocese, and in 1788 it involved 51% of the parishes[32]. The replies to the bishop's visitation in 1765 given above show that this was happening locally, and a curate from Romsey was taking services in both Lockerley and Romsey. However, most parish parsons lived reasonably well, and some had a lifestyle similar to a country gentleman. As the lord of the manor usually had the right of presentation to the local parish living, he often used it as a career opportunity for one of his younger sons, and in the 19th century frequently provided a large Victorian parsonage to house him. Such clergymen sometimes spent rather more of their time on country sports than on their parish duties, of which one of the more famous examples was the West Country clergyman, the Rev. John Russell, who spent most of his time in the hunting field and whose lasting memorial is the short-legged Jack Russell terrier which he developed for going down fox holes more easily. Other country parsons had rather more academic interests, and G.S. Master, rector of West Dean, devoted his time to archaeology and history. He excavated the remains of the Roman villa in West Dean, and wrote his 'Collections for a history of West Dean', for which he amassed a vast amount of historical information. Another parson with active 'outside' interests was Gilbert White, the celebrated naturalist and author of The Natural History of Selborne, who was curate in West Dean for a time during the 1750s.

Nonconformity

During the second half of the 18th century Nonconformity progressively gathered momentum. It was the era of the great preacher, particularly John Wesley, who preached around Salisbury in the 1740s, and in 1750 the first Wesleyan-Methodist chapel was opened in Salisbury. Methodism spread from the towns out into and around the countryside, particularly among the older dissenting sects, and there was a corresponding reduction in Presbyterianism and the Quakers. There was a considerable expansion of the Baptists during the first half of the 19th century, and although the

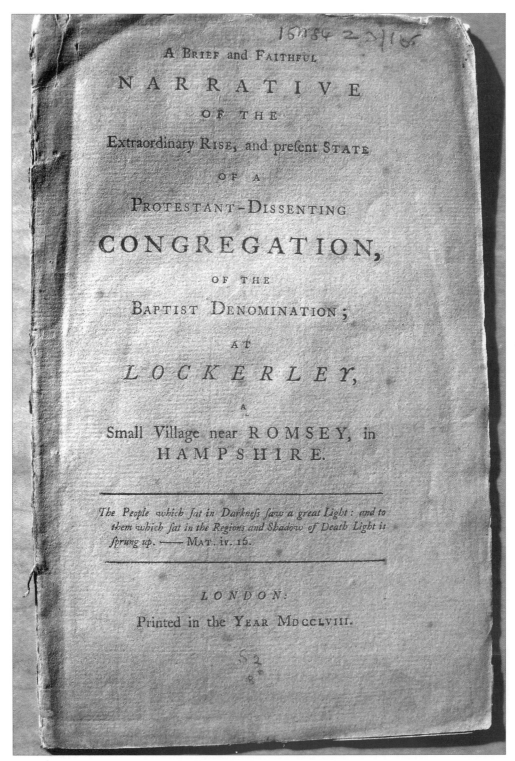

Fig. 14 *Booklet on Lockerley Baptist church, 1758. HRO ref.15M84/ Z3/165 (AB)*

number of Baptist chapels in the towns increased, much of the expansion was in rural areas. However, the greatest proliferation in the 19th century was in the various Methodist groups, and they established chapels in many of the villages. These were often in hamlets away from the centre of the parish, perhaps where the influence of the parish church was felt less strongly, or where there was only a visiting Anglican curate who did not have a very strong presence. There were two different associations of Methodists, the Wesleyan and the Primitive Methodists, and their preachers often travelled round a circuit of small chapels. The earliest chapels were often very small, or even cottages, but many were later expanded and refitted.

A religious census conducted in 1851 shows the relative numbers of churches and Nonconformist chapels in the Hampshire countryside. Stockbridge district, which included West Dean with its chapel at East Grimstead, recorded the following[33]:

Church of England	14	places of worship
Baptist	3	
Soc. of Friends (Quakers)	1	
Wesleyan Methodists	3	
Primitive Methodists	5	
Wesleyan Association	3	

Both the Baptists and the Primitive Methodists built chapels in Lockerley. Some of the people in the parish became influenced by the Baptist movement and had visiting pastors to preach to them, particularly Mr. Fanch of Romsey. Cottage meetings commenced in 1751 and a church was formed in 1752. A larger building was then acquired and furnished as a meeting house and was registered in 1757. Nearly a hundred years later, in 1844, a Primitive Methodist Chapel was founded in Newtown, a hamlet in Lockerley parish, and the census in 1851 showed that while the Baptists had an average attendance at services of 88, the Methodists had 108. The average attendance at the parish church for comparison was 163, which shows that Nonconformism was of considerable importance in the area, but that all three religious communities were coexisting and in a fairly viable state at that time[34]. Both West Dean and East Grimstead also had Methodist chapels in the 19th century.

The Methodists realised the power and pleasure of singing communally, and introduced the singing of hymns, many of which were produced by the great hymn writers Charles Wesley and Isaac Watts. Music and the singing of hymns during services were also gradually introduced into the parish churches, which had previously had very limited singing, and that only psalm singing by a choir, not the congregation. Groups of village musicians and choirs of singers who led the congregation became commonplace in country churches, and west-end galleries were often built to accommodate them.

Harmony Hall, East Tytherley

The rapid rate of development of capitalist industrialization during the 19th century left many people with an uneasy feeling that something was missing, and that the old integration between town and country had been lost. Some looked backwards to the medieval community, seeing only its stability and virtues, while forgetting the hierarchical society, the constraints of the established church and the perpetual problem of poverty. Long-past societies such as the monastic communities began to be viewed in an idealistic light, as representing small-scale cooperative communities. The expression of this developing concept took a variety of different forms, one of which was the alternative community. There were many experiments in group living and a leading exponent was the early socialist, Robert Owen, who had plans for a radically different type of society. Britain would become a nation of small villages again rather than large industrialized cities, although recent developments in industrial machinery would be incorporated and put to good use. There would be education for both adults and children, and everyone would share both the work-load and the profits. Poverty would be eliminated.

One such alternative community was developed on the edge of East Tytherley parish. It was the only community to be sponsored directly by the official Owenite organisation, who leased 530 acres of land in the Queenwood part of East Tytherley, and a piece of land in the adjacent extra-parochial area of Buckholt, from Sir Isaac Goldsmid in 1839 and the first settlers arrived soon afterwards. They came from Owenite branches in northern industrial towns, and with very little knowledge of agriculture, were immediately plunged into a farming existence with scant help or guidance. Winter came, and the community struggled with unfamiliar work, crowded conditions and poor health. As a consequence the community shrank from 57 to 19 in 1840. Owen himself took up residence in 1841, and with no expense spared, had a grandiose new building constructed on the site to

QUEENWOOD COLLEGE,

FOUR MILES FROM DUNBRIDGE STATION, SOUTH-WESTERN RAILWAY,

HAMPSHIRE.

THE COURSE OF INSTRUCTION EMBRACES—

MATHEMATICS, NATURAL PHILOSOPHY, THEORETIC AND PRACTICAL CHEMISTRY,
ENGLISH, CLASSICS, FOREIGN LANGUAGES,
PRACTICAL SURVEYING, LEVELLING, &c., MECHANICAL AND FREE-HAND DRAWING,
AND MUSIC.

THE PRINCIPAL IS ASSISTED BY TEN RESIDENT MASTERS.

The position of the Establishment is healthful, and the advantages various and unusual.

Attention is invited to the Prospectus, which may be had on application.

The next half-year will commence on July 31st, 1862.

TERMS—

Including the use of Books, except such as a Pupil may require for his exclusive use, and of Philosophical Apparatus.

For Boys under 12 years of Age	£45 per annum.
Ditto from 12 to 15	55 „
Ditto above 15	65 „

Laundress and Sempstress, Three Pounds per annum. Chemical Apparatus and Tests and Lessons in Instrumental Music, are Extras.

Payments to be made Quarterly, in advance, to GEORGE EDMONDSON, Queenwood.

A Quarter's Notice required prior to the removal of a Pupil.

c

Fig. 15   *Extract from London Society Advertiser, 1862. HRO ref. 27A04/5 (AB)*

house the residents and to create a new school. The result was Harmony Hall, a three-storey brick building with 80 rooms (Fig.XIV, p51). Owen also extended the estate to about 1000 acres by taking leases on Great and Little Bentley farms and Rose Hill (now Hildon House); Rose Hill House became accommodation for some of the community. By 1843 there were 45 adults and 25 children. The farming enterprise, after the initial difficulties, thrived and the community obtained good yields from their crops. New ideas about how to increase agricultural productivity were used to good effect, particularly the application of manure to improve the fertility of the thin chalk soil.

This socialist enterprise, with its flamboyant building, attracted a certain amount of suspicion and criticism from the outside world, but its total collapse in 1845 was brought about by financial failure and the threat of bankruptcy, rather than local opposition to the community[35].

The imposing, but now redundant, building, with its spacious accommodation designed for community living, provided the ideal premises for a school. George Edmondson, a school master who had been brought up in the Quaker tradition, and had already established a successful school in Blackburn, was persuaded by the Owenites in 1847 that it would be the right place to carry out his 'enlarged views of education'. His school, which became known as Queenwood College, was a success and soon had 90 boys as pupils. The school prospectus of 1862 advertised:

English, Modern Languages, Mathematics, Drawing and Music. Queenwood College is especially famous for its science teaching. Great encouragement is given to the collections in Entomology, Ornithology, Botany, Carpentering, Taxidermy, Microscopy and Photography. The evening lectures are well illustrated by experiment and diagrams, a great feature of the college course. On leisure evenings there are entertainments and lectures by the boys.

Queenwood College continued to be successful for a time, and its more notable pupils included Henry Fawcett, the blind Postmaster General, whose imposing statue stands in Salisbury's Market Square. However, by the 1890s the school had lost popularity and it was closed in 1896. Unfortunately, the building was burnt down in 1902, and so very little remains as a reminder of Robert Owen's experiment in the alternative lifestyle[36].

6
Probate Inventories

The probate inventory provided an official list of the value of a person's movable goods and chattels at death which was needed to prove the will and for the payment of creditors; land was not included. The inventories provide an interesting insight into the lives of people in past centuries, particularly those from the 16th and 17th centuries which give considerable detail, and often include what we would regard today as very trivial items. What stands out is how few possessions even relatively wealthy people had.

A Statute of Henry VIII in 1529 regularised what had by then become a common custom and laid down how it was to be carried out. The executor of the will, or when the deceased had died intestate, an appointed administrator, had to provide an inventory of the goods and their value, assessed by at least two other persons. These 'appraisers' were to be creditors of the deceased, or persons to whom he had made a legacy; when this was not applicable relatives or other honest persons were to be appointed. Many appraisers were illiterate and could only sign the inventory with their mark but this did not mean that they were not aware of the value of the goods. Respected members of the community, such as farmers, craftsmen and tradesmen were quite frequently not literate, but were able to participate fully in the functioning of the local parish or town, acting for example as churchwardens or overseers of the poor. Probate inventories were required until 1859.

The inventory listed all the movable goods and chattels owned by a person at death. As houses became larger and had more contents it became harder to draw the distinction between fixtures belonging to the landlord, and fittings which were the movable property of the deceased. Window glass, a luxury at a time when smaller houses had only oiled cloth or horn covering the window when the shutters were drawn back, was at one time classed as movable goods. In addition, domestic equipment merged into industrial scale fixtures as small local businesses grew larger. Typical examples include the 'furnace', a big copper built into a solid base with its own fire for washing or brewing in the home; Dun Valley inventories frequently list such furnaces. On a larger scale they become industrial equipment as used by dyers and brewers and were no longer regarded as movable. The cheese press, which also appears on our local inventories, similarly became a fixture when very large[1]. Movable goods included household items, standing and stored crops, domestic livestock including poultry and bees, and money owed to the deceased. In the days before banks people with money to spare frequently provided loans around the local community, both as bonds and as 'desperate debts' or unsecured loans, and such loans often made up a substantial proportion of the deceased's estate.

Some limitations have to be taken into account when assessing the lists of belongings. It is a list of what a person owned at death, and there is therefore likely to be a difference between the goods of a person dying suddenly while still actively farming or running a business, and a person who has lingered into old age and has already handed on some of his cattle and sheep to his sons, or who has given up riding his horse some years previously. There are also seasonal variations to take into account, standing crops and numbers of growing lambs will be greater during the summer months, stored corn will be greater after the harvest, and surplus animals, which were normally sold or killed in the autumn, appear as stored salted carcases hanging 'at the roof' in the winter. Nevertheless, when large numbers of inventories are studied and comparisons are made with those from other areas, a wealth of information can be gleaned about life in the past, particularly in Tudor and Stuart times when inventories were very detailed.

Forty four inventories from the Dun Valley parishes were examined in detail[2], a list of which is given in Appendix I. Within the constraints of what had survived and what was legible, inventories from a time span of 150 years were examined, including those from people of as many different occupations as possible. The total value is also given where possible.

The probate inventories provide useful information, not only about the contents of the houses during the 16th and 17th centuries, but also about the construction of the buildings themselves. The medieval houses would have been timber-framed with wattle and daub infill and a thatched roof; originally just single-story, one-roomed dwellings. During the 16th century these gradually expanded into more robust buildings, although of similar construction, divided into separate rooms and often having an upper story, and by 1600 most houses had more than two rooms and usually had two stories.

Brick was increasingly used for chimneys to reduce the risk of fire, and it gradually became more popular in house construction, particularly when timber became scarce in some areas of the country. It also reduced the risk of fire in towns. Around the Dun Valley, however, there was extensive woodland producing both oak for timber and hazel coppice for the wattle infill, and timber-framed buildings continued to be built. The use of brick in the region gradually increased, helped by the fact that there were good local deposits of suitable clay, and by the 18th century even modest cottages in the district were brick-built.

There would also have been some chalk-walled cottages from very early times, using the chalk from the various chalk pits around. It was a cheap and simple way of building a cottage, which could be carried out by the cottager himself with a few simple tools. However, the Dun Valley is not on the chalk downland and although there is plenty of chalk available, there are extensive areas of other soil types, unlike villages a few miles further north in Wiltshire and Hampshire, where chalk was dug out of the ground on site, forming a cellar below the house, and no transport was required.

The simply-constructed small houses and cottages of past centuries were not expected to last indefinitely, even the substantial ones were frequently destroyed by fire. The old timber-framed cottages which can be seen in the villages today were the larger, well constructed homes of the better-off members of the local society, particularly the houses of yeoman farmers, merchants and tradesmen. They have been extensively renovated over the past 400 years, while lesser cottages have long since fallen down or been demolished. Stone was not available anywhere in the locality and was not used as a routine building material; even the churches originally had chalk and rubble walls.

The timber-framed house in the 13th and 14th centuries was a simple one-roomed building with a central hearth and no chimney; the smoke drifted out through a hole in the roof. Life gradually became more comfortable as the inner space was sub-divided into separate rooms with different functions. The earliest subdivision formed a smoke bay at one end, from which the gable-end chimney developed. Later, during the 16th century chimney stacks were built centrally between the hall and parlour. Partitioning off the upper part of the wall, with the fire placed behind it, drew the smoke away from the room, and gradually developed into the large inglenook fireplace still seen in old houses today. Originally everyone lived, ate and slept within the one main room, known as the 'hall', but further

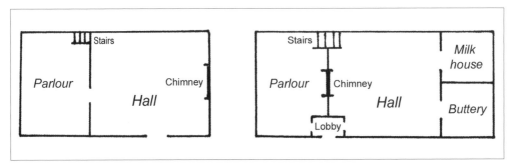

Fig. 16 *Typical ground plans of 16th century farm houses.(MB)*

subdivisions of the spaces between the main supporting posts followed the chimney bay, and this provided separate chambers which allowed some degree of privacy. It also made separate working areas for some of the household tasks. Additional accommodation was provided by boarding over the roof space to form a loft, which later developed into an upper story. At first access was by a simple ladder, which later became a staircase. Adding an upper story to a house required a stronger, better constructed, building, and such houses were built by skilled carpenters rather than the owner with local unskilled help. The frames of the house were cut in the carpenter's yard and marked before being transported to the house site for erection[3]. The typical ground floor layout of simple 16th and 17th century houses is shown in Fig. 16. Particularly good examples of a range of houses from the 17th century can be seen at the Weald and Downland Open Air Museum, Singleton, Chichester, Sussex.

The hall

The main living room was referred to as the 'hall' and daily life took place there; in earlier times there would have been no other rooms. The fire was in the hall, originally in a hearth in the centre of the room, but from about 1500 onwards a fireplace and chimney above became increasingly common. The hall was normally the only heated room in the house and was where the cooking took place. (Figs.XV, XVI, p54).

The probate inventories often give an indication of how the house was arranged as the individual rooms are named and the contents listed separately. About half of the inventories examined refer to the separate rooms, the rest simply list everything together. The contents of the hall usually included an 'unjoined' or trestle table, a form and 1 or 2 chairs. Included in many inventories were a number of brass and pewter items, such as pots, platters or candlesticks. These were regarded as valuable and they were handed down in families, often being donated personally in wills. Thomas Dangerfield of East Dean made it very clear who was to get which piece in his will:

I give to Edmund, my eldest son, my best brasse pott, my best brasse pan and the three best dishes or pieces of my best pewter. I give unto my son John my second brasse pott, my best kettle and three next best dishes or pieces of pewter. I give to my son Richard my third best brasse pott and three pieces of the next best pewter. I give to Dorathye, my eldest daughter, my forth best brasse pott and three dishes or pieces of my next best pewter. I give to Elizabeth my daughter my fifth best brasse pott and three dishes or pieces of my next best pewter.

Everyday meals were eaten off wooden trenchers or platters, while more liquid gruels and stews were contained in porringers. Spoons are sometimes mentioned but knives are few in number and were for cutting while preparing the food. Forks were not used at all. Cooking utensils are listed in the hall together with the fireside equipment and include kettles, cauldrons, frying pans, sieves, chafing dishes and skillets. The pots and kettles were held in place by pot hooks and hangers. There was often a spit or broche, andirons and trivets.

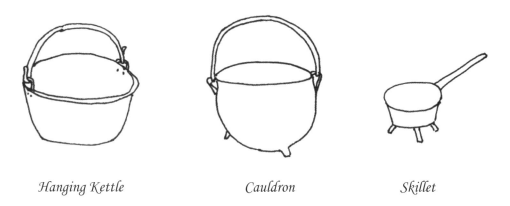

Hanging Kettle   *Cauldron*   *Skillet*

Andirons: metal bars which support the logs on the fire, also called fire dogs.
Chafing dish: a metal box holding burning coal or charcoal, used for heating food gently.
Skillet: a long-handled pan with 3 short legs which sat directly on the fire.

There were also flitches of bacon hanging from the roof in many of the homes, gradually being smoked following curing with salt. Many outdoor implements and boxes of stored items were listed as being in the hall, but this may, or may not, reflect what had been there during the owner's lifetime; it would be likely that things were moved about after his death. Most of the items listed were of a very functional nature, but better-off households had tablecloths and napkins which must have softened the very Spartan effect, even if they were only used on special occasions. They also decorated their walls with 'painted cloths' or pictures on canvas. Lighting would have been low-level at best, the firelight supplemented with candles in some cases, while less well-off families probably made do with rush lights, which are not included separately in inventories. One lantern is mentioned.

Other rooms

Many of the inventories indicate that the house had more rooms than just the principal living room or hall. Some of the extra rooms provided sleeping areas and a degree of privacy for members of the family and are variously described as:

The loft over the hall, the chamber above stairs, the inchamber, the outchamber, the servants chamber, the parlour, the other chamber

Some houses were small and simple, just the hall and the chamber, while others had several rooms. Part, or all, of the house may have been open to the roof, but many houses had lofts over some or all of the rooms which were reached by a ladder or staircase. The chamber contained the bed, or beds, and coffers or chests to hold the linen and clothes. Sometimes there was also a cupboard, but little else except stored items, and by modern standards the rooms would have appeared sparsely furnished. However, there was often an attempt to make a room appear more attractive by having wall hangings, and the 'cloths' around a four poster bed would have added to the effect. Robert Tutt of Lockerley had a rug, and William Ireland of East Dean had a chair in each of his bedchambers. Only Augustine Betteridge of Lockerley had a chamber pot on his inventory; presumably others had similar containers but they were not considered worth itemising.

The bedsteads were usually wooden, and the best bed was often a four poster with a tester, or canopy, from which curtains were hung to keep out the draughts. A truckle bed, which pushed underneath the bedstead, and could then be pulled out as required, is occasionally mentioned (Fig.XVIII, p55). Robert Tutt, a gentleman, had truckle beds in each of his bedrooms, in addition to his four post bed with curtains and three other beds. Truckle beds were used for servants who slept in their master or mistress's room. Mattresses, bolsters and pillows were of either feather or flock, and it was always specified which on the inventory as the value of feather beds was greater than flock ones. Often the best bed was feather, the others flock. The bed 'linen' consisted of linen, canvas or lockram (coarse linen) sheets, and in addition there were blankets and coverlets. When the family had tablecloths and napkins these were stored with the sheets.

Other rooms in the larger houses provided space where the food and drink could be prepared and stored instead of in the hall. Much time and effort went into preserving meat, turning the milk into butter and cheese and brewing the ale, and the produce all had to be stored somewhere afterwards. The rooms are variously described as the buttery, the kitchen, the bake house, the milk house, the cheesepress house, the malt house or the brew house. 'House' in this context could be a separate building but often only implies a separate room. John Russon of Lockerley had an oriel, an upper gallery or partial loft, used for similar functions.

Meat was preserved by salting the carcase, usually a pig, over a long time. It was carried out in a trough large enough to hold a side, or flitch, and salt was rubbed into the flesh for several weeks. Afterwards the bacon was sometimes smoked by hanging it in the large chimney place above the wood fire. It then had to be hung somewhere until required for use. The inventories frequently include one or two flitches of bacon, while some of the larger households had large numbers '10 flitches of bacon' or '5 hogs of bacon' in the kitchen, which must have taken up considerable space. So too must the 'powdering troughs' used for salting, which are also often mentioned.

The traditional drink was ale or beer and large quantities of it were brewed in the home. Until hops were available ale did not keep for long and it had to be brewed frequently. There was no coffee or tea and the water would frequently have been unpalatable.

The first part of the brewing process was to convert barley into malt. Barley grains were steeped in water for three days before being drained and encouraged to sprout. At that stage the barley was referred to as malt. The malt was dried, winnowed and ground and was then ready for brewing. Water was added to the ground malt and it was left to stand, after which the 'wort' was drained off. When hops were used they were boiled in the wort and then removed. The addition of hops makes beer, rather than ale, which keeps longer. The ale or beer was cleared, clay was often used for this, before it was put into barrels[4]. The process was quite a long one and would have taken up a lot of space, especially if the house was a small one without a separate malt or brewhouse. The inventories contain many references to brewing equipment such as quernes to grind malt, and barrels.

Cheese and butter making was another process which took place in the home. Milk does not keep very long in its original state and preserving it as cheese and butter would have been an ongoing task during the summer months when most of the milk was produced. Butter churns and cheese vats were commonplace in the inventories in such rooms as the milkhouse, buttery or kitchen. The stored cheeses then had to be accommodated until they were used or sold, and one of the larger houses had a 'cheeseloft'.

Milk Maid

Clothes

In most of the inventories the clothes of the deceased are just described collectively as 'his wearing apparel'. Fortunately in some cases a detailed description is given, which when the inventories are taken together creates a picture of how the men in country areas dressed in Tudor and Stuart times.

Some examples are given below:

1563 *Richard Lodge, cleric*
1 short gown of black lined black cotton & the fore quarters lined with worsted, 1 short gown lined with black cotton, 1 long gown lined with black cotton, 1 other gown of bristow, 1 new black cotton coat, 1 chamlet jacket, 1 typatt of taffeta, 1 black fustian doublet & 1 ... doublet, 3 pairs of hose, 1 new red petticoat, 4 shirts

1573   Hugh Hatcher, husbandman
1 black coat, 3 jerkins, 3 pairs of hose, 1 cap, 1 russet cloak, 2 pairs of shoes, 1 pair of boots

1581   William Canterton, gent
A taffeta hat, a felt and a straw hat, a green coat, a cloak in pieces, 2 old night caps in velvet, 2 shirts, 2 pairs boots & buskins, 2 garters, 1 scarf, a quilted fustian doublet, a shirt, 1 canvas doublet, a leather jerkin, an old cloak, a wastle

1582   Robert Gynes, husbandman
1 cloak, 3 pairs of gaskins, 1 jerkin, 1 doublet, 3 shirts, 1 hat

1594   John Russon, senior
2 doublets, 1 pair of russet stockings, 2 russet jerkins, 1 pair russet breeches, 1 russet cloak

1694   Thomas Gilbert
2 suits of wearing apparel and his linen, 2 pairs of boots

Buskins:	high boots worn by country folk
Chamlet	(camlet:) a fabric of mixed silk, wool and hair
Fustian:	cloth of mixed cotton and flax
Gaskins	(galligaskins): loose hose
Typatt	(tippet): a shoulder cape
Wastle	(wastel:) originally bread baked from the finest wheat, used heraldically for a round cake used as a bearing. Here possibly used to describe a round hat.

Other items

Many of the bits and pieces in peoples' homes were small and of little value. The appraisers simply added them together, referred to them as '*other lumber*' and gave them a nominal value.

Literacy

Many of the villagers would not have been able to read or write before the 19th century and it was not unusual for the appraisers of the inventories to sign the document with their mark instead of a signature. Very few of the lists of belongings include books. Clerics were literate and both Edward Blackford and Robert Wheatley had 'books', the use of the plural suggests that they had quite a number. Two or three of the yeomen farmers had a bible and a couple of other books and Robert Tutt, gent, had books worth £5. For Christopher Dobbs, surgeon, the description is '*all his books*' and they were likely to have been the books of remedies and recipes for the medicines which were available at that time.

Farm Animals

Although one would expect the inventories of yeoman farmers and husbandmen to include farm livestock, their ownership was much wider. In rural areas in the 16th and 17th centuries most people above the very poorest section of society expected to be fairly self-sufficient and had at least a few animals and a large vegetable garden. Even very modest cottages had a small area of enclosed land as well as common grazing rights for their animals on the manorial 'waste' (rough grazing land and woodland) and on the arable land after the harvest.

Cattle

Cows were originally kept to produce the draught oxen, but this function had gradually diminished by Tudor and Stuart times. Oxen, the castrated male cattle used for pulling the plough and general haulage, are mentioned only three times in the inventories, all in the late 16th century. William Canterton had a team of four, Steven Fox had two and John Russon had three. By the 16th century horses had taken over from oxen for most of the farm work, they were more adaptable and better at pulling loads on light ground or roads. However, oxen pulled the plough better on heavy, sticky clay ground, and well-off farmers, such as Canterton and Russon, who could afford to keep oxen in addition to horses no doubt found them still useful. Cows were by that date mainly kept to supply milk for making into butter and cheese. Milk is a very perishable product and most of it had to be preserved in some way. The volume of milk which a cow produced at that time would not have been very great by modern standards, and the calf would have taken some of it. Cows were only milked during the summer months and were dried off while in-calf during the winter, when food was scarce. Cattle numbers are quite low in the inventories, ranging from one or two to a maximum of twenty. This includes half-grown heifers and steers but not the calves.

Sheep

Sheep numbers were small when compared with chalk-downland parishes; Thomas Dangerfield, a yeoman farmer, had 220, which was the highest number. This is to be expected in a region of mainly woodland and low-lying ground. In East Tytherley even the lord of the manor had only 652 ewes in 1680[5], which is very different from the huge sheep flocks which grazed the Hampshire and Wiltshire downland.   In addition to wool production ewes' milk was used to make cheese. Both cows' and ewes' milk was used for butter and cheese, and the milk of both species was often mixed together. Much of the butter was whey butter, made as a by-product of cheese production, rather than made from whole milk. According to late medieval calculations one cow gave about as much milk as ten ewes[6].

Pigs

Many people kept a few pigs to provide the bacon which was part of the staple fare of all households. Although they were given some corn to fatten them, they could utilise household waste such as the washings of ale barrels and whey from cheese making.

Horses

Fig. 17 *Carthorse. (T. Bewick)*

About half of the inventories include one or more horses and there is often some indication from the equipment listed of the type of horse, for example plough harness as opposed to a saddle and bridle. It is probably also a fair assumption that a farmer had mainly carthorses, and not surprisingly the indications are that the parsons and the surgeon had riding horses. Sometimes there is a slightly more informative description, William Canterton had a grey gelding called Fish, presumably originally purchased from a Mr. Fish, and a grey 'curtal' or dock-tailed horse. The latter suggests that although docking was probably common for cart horses, where the tail could get tangled up with the reins, a docked riding horse was sufficiently unusual to deserve listing separately. Horses were valuable as they formed a considerable part of the farmer's wealth, and unlike oxen, were not turned into meat when their working days were over. The more affluent yeomen farmers had about five horses, whereas other villagers kept just one or two. The inclusion of a 'saddle and pillion' in the inventory of a gentleman, Robert Tutt, is a reminder that ladies in the 17th century ladies sometimes rode up behind.

Poultry are listed on ten of the inventories and include cocks, hens, geese and ducks. The numbers given are very small, a common finding in rural probate inventories, and it has been suggested that they were usually under-reported as they were hard to find and count[7]. Eight of the inventories mention bees, usually only two or three 'beestalls' or hives, but Nicholas Blake of East Dean was involved in more extensive production with seven. Rabbits, fish and pigeons were not included in inventories so that no information can be gained from them about the part these sources of food played in the local diet.

Farm Equipment

Many of the inventories, particularly those of the yeomen farmers and husbandmen, included the implements necessary for all the various farming activities. Most of them had the smaller hand tools such as scythes, axes, bills and hatchets, while the larger farmers also had ploughs, harrows, carts and wagons.

Stored Goods and Standing Crops

Stored goods were principally the produce of the land kept to provide food for the family household and also winter feed for the farm animals when grass was scarce. Some may also have been kept to go for sale at the markets. Commonly stored items included corn, malt, bacon, hops, cheeses, hay, wool and wood. Twelve of the inventories have no stored goods at all. Cereal crops made up the main bulk and included wheat, barley, rye and oats and there were also smaller quantities of peas. Malt was commonly listed because ale, and later beer, were frequently brewed in the home. The introduction of hops as a crop, which when included in the mixture made beer rather than ale, greatly improved the keeping qualities and enabled brewing to be carried out on a larger scale. Two of the bigger farmers, William Ireland and Thomas Dangerfield, both of East Dean, had stored hops among their goods.

Five inventories included cheeses, one of which, that of John Moore, had ten cheeses, possibly indicating production for sale. His cow herd contained a fairly modest five cows and he had no sheep.

Bacon, usually as flitches (sides) hanging 'at the roof', was the principal form of stored meat in all types of household and only one inventory included preserved beef. Animal fat was another valuable stored item, '2 gallons of grease' and 6lbs of lard are both given in the Dun Valley inventories. It was used not only for cooking but also for rush lights, the common form of lighting. Mutton fat burned cleanest and brightest, and an even better light could be produced by the addition of beeswax. Skimmings of the bacon pot provided a cheaper but less good alternative[8].

Some of the stored produce was winter feed for the animals. Oats were grown for horse food and some of the barley and peas would have been destined for the cattle and pigs. Vetches, plants in the pea family which were used both as green food and dried as a form of hay, appear on a few inventories. Hay was made particularly for the horses. Interestingly straw never appears as such in inventories; it was obviously included in the list of stored corn before threshing, but afterwards the straw must have been stored as food and bedding for all the farm animals, and straw for thatching would have been important. Probate inventories did not include crops the harvesting of which involved breaking up the ground, root crops are therefore excluded. Stored apples were included, but not fruit while it was still growing on the tree, presumably it would have been hard to put a price on it at that stage.

The list of standing crops is similar to that of the stored ones. The acreages when they are given are small and represent some of the strips in the open fields belonging to the deceased. Approximately a third of the arable land was left fallow each year which considerably reduced the annual crop, and as mentioned above, the time of the year would make a considerable difference to the quantity in the ground.

Other products which were stored included wool from the sheep and wood, which meant boards or timber for building or furniture repairs rather than just firewood.

Military Equipment

Some of the most interesting objects listed in the inventories are the weapons and military equipment.

1565 *Richard Lodge, cleric*
2 bows with ye bow case of leather, 10 arrows in a quiver

1581 *William Canterton, gent*
2 daggers

1582 *Robert Gynes, husbandman*
1 girdle and a dagger, a bow and 6 arrows

1592 *William Ireland*
1 bow and a bill, furnished

1594 *John Russon*
A watche bill, a sword, a scull and a cap for muster, a long bow and a sheaf of arrows for muster

1629 *George Fox, yeoman*
1 musket

1638 *Robert Tutt, gent*
A caliver and pistol, one old corslet

1638 *Richard Bonner, yeoman*
1 furnished corslet and a pike

1638 *Richard Bennet*
A Welch bill, 1 holbert

1669 *Christopher Dobbs, surgeon*
Guns, pistols, swords, armour viz back, breast and
headpiece, and a troop saddle

Caliver: a light kind of musket, fired without a rest
Corslet (corselet):   body armour
Furnished: ready for use
Holbert (halberd):   a combination of an axe and a spear

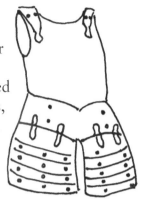

During the 16th century all able-bodied men were expected
to practise using the longbow on Sundays and holidays,
usually on the village open common land, and Elizabeth
I tried to maintain a state of preparedness for war with
these trained bands of local militia. However, by 1600
it had long been recognised that other weapons had
superseded the longbow and during the early 17th
century men were required to 'furnish' themselves with
arms appropriate to their social status when summoned

Military Corslet
and Helmet

to attend muster. The trained bands were under the supervision of the lord
lieutenant of the shire, who was responsible for arranging periodic musters,
officially four times a year during the summer months. One Hampshire
muster which would have involved the Dun Valley villages was held in
1602. Hampden Powlett, the lord lieutenant, wrote to his cousin Sir Henry
Whitehead of Norman Court, West Tytherley as follows[9]:

Cousin Whithed .... these are to let you understand that I have appointed
to muster and view your said company at or near the Beech called Whitway
Beech near Broughton under Buckholt Hill on Wednesday next ...

The local militia continued until everyone became caught up in the civil
war. The muster book of Richard Whitehead esq. for *c* 1632 includes the
following names from local villages[10]:

Richard Whithed his company

Corslets

<u>West Tuderly</u> *Edward Rogers, Edward Ree, Henry Prangnell by ye tything,*
Richard Carpenter, Thomas Dangerfeild, Thomas Fox by ye tything of
East Deane.

East Tuderly   Damell Knight, Silvester Woodford, George Langredg, George Garret, Edward Dangerfeild, George Bonner.

Muskets

West Tuderly   Thomas Aldredg, William Rogers, Augustine Wilton, John Bettredg, James Burges, Robert Geffory, Robert Turner, Roger Southwell, Walter Kent, Richard Terry, Henry Kerry.

Tools of the trade

A few of the inventories included what might be termed tools of the trade.

Silvester Langridge, blacksmith,   furnice

Christopher Dobbs, surgeon,   glass bottles, vials, gally pots and glasses, surgical instruments and lances, scales, mortar and pestle, a press glass (glass cupboard) and other small things in it, books

T homas Hatcher, carpenter,   carpenter's tools

Edward Hinxman, blacksmith,   firepan and tongs

John Hobbs, butcher,   pole axe, ...ting knifes, hand hook, double crooks, beams and scales, the weights in ye shop, ropes, blocks, stool, tray, bucket

George Ventham, yeoman,   had a shop and tools but unfortunately there is no indication as to what he produced or repaired.

Dr Dobbs of East Tytherley also had a still, the apparatus for brewing spirits, which in the 17th century was likely to have been for medicinal purposes, although he may have realised that spirits made his patients feel better, even if he could not cure the disease. Dobbs appears in several parish records of the 1650s and 60s, so a little more can be deduced about the life of a rural surgeon of that time. In 1655 he was the tythingman for East Tytherley and was present as part of the jury at the manor court at intervals over several years. In the hearth tax of 1665 he had two fairly small properties, one in East Tytherley and one in Lockerley and he was a leaseholder, a man of reasonable standing in the community but modest means. Interestingly there is a record of a purchase of leeches from Mrs Dobbs in 1680[11], presumably she had retained a small part of his work after his death.

In general, where people had crops and farm animals these were a large part of the value of their movable goods and chattels at death; the household goods when added together were far less so. The other items on some of the inventories which often accounted for a considerable proportion of the total wealth was money lent to other villagers, or debts to be recovered.

The inventory of John Moore of East Tytherley includes *'dettes due unto hym'*, a list of small loans to local people. Robert Wheatley, cleric of East Dean, had £20 worth of *'debts good and desperate'* included in his total wealth of £43. Good debts were money lent as bonds or similar, desperate debts were unsecured loans. Movable goods did not include land, but did include the unexpired part of a lease where land was held by leasehold tenure. John Kent and Richard Vaughan, both yeomen, had leases on their inventories, but most of the land was held by copyhold tenure which was inherited through the manor court (see chap 7).

The inventories of the three widows were not significantly different from those of the men. Women could continue to hold and work their former husband's farm, and much of the indoor work, such as making cheese and brewing, would always have been carried out by them anyway. Both Eleanor and Agnes Pragnell had crops and farm animals; Margery Ireland had household items only, together with money in bonds.

The inventories cover a time period of over 150 years, from Elizabethan times until well after the civil war and into the 18th century, but there is very little change in the nature of people's worldly goods over the time investigated. Three of the inventories are reproduced below as examples:

1591B/66 John Prangnell of East Tytherley   1591

The wheat in the feilde	*£3 13s 4d*
The otes in the felde	*24s*
The pezen (peas) & fetches (vetches)	*40s*
In cattell four kyne	*£5 5s 8d*
Nyne bullucks	*£5*

2 *hors (horses)* & *a little colt*	*40s*
Half a hundred of shepe	*£8 6s 8d*
In woll	*33s 4d*
A chest, a bedsted & a coffer	*13s 4d*
A fat (vat), 2 barrelles, a pan, thre candlestyks, four pewter dyshes & 2	
sacks	*10s 4d*
One hundred of dry bordes, a peyr of eyther (harrows) & som wod in the	
barton	*10s*
His apparel	*20s*
Total £31 17s 8d	

His debts owing unto sayd testators be apon the wyll ....

1597A/63 John Moore, husbandman, of East Tytherley 1597

Hys apparel	*20s*
16 platters, sevin pottengers, 3 sawsers, 4 pewter dysshs, 4 salts and a	
pewter pott	*33s 4d*
5 candelstycks	*2s 8d*
Five brasse panes	*40s*
2 furnyses, 3 skylletts, a chafyng dyshe, 3 kyttles	*36s*
Five brasse potts	*40s*

*A paire of pothooks, five? cotterells, an yron bolt in the chimney with
2 iron pynnes, a grydyron, 3 ..., 4 iron wedges, 3 cleavinge knyves,
a chopping kniff, two axes, 3 bylls, 2 mattocks, an yron barre, a shoinge,
a pickax, a tunell, 2 hatchettes, a hooke, 2 payre of ploughirons, a plow
chayne, 3 pranges, a forest byll 2 fryinge panes, 2 syths, 4 riphookes,
4 bryers, 2 ch...ylls, 2 adses, a handsawe with 2 wymbles (drills)*   *35s*

*A sty..., one dozen of tym..n spones, 4 parie of sheepe shears, ... of
woodden dysshes, 3 stone cuppes, a potte & an yron beame for weightes*

10s

*Syx barrels, 2 covelles (tubs) a busshell, a peck, 2 trendles, a well bucket,
2 other buckettes and 2 tubbes*   *25s*

*One fetherbed, three bolsters, fyve coverlettes, 2 parie of blankettes,
2 parie of sheets, 2 pyllowes, one tester, 2 board clothes and 3 bedsteeds*

£5 13s 4d

One chest and 5 cofers	*15s*
Syx stayned (painted) clothes old & a tester stayned	*10s*
One sylt, one powdrynge tube and a butter churne	*8s*

3 olde sawes and old yron in a loft   26s 8d
A cowbard (cupboard), a table board, one joined forme, 2 benches,
5 shelffs and 4 weight of led   12s
wheat in the barne and winnowed in the house, 2 quarters worth
                                                                                     £10 16s
Syx quarters and ... of barley worth   £15 8s 8d
3 quarters malt worth   £7 4s 4d
12 bushells of pease worth   72s
Twelve hundred of board worth   £4
One yron bound cart, one newe paire of wheeles, one plough and
4 eythes   60s
The horse harnes and a well bucket   10s
Syx sackes worth   10s
A hear, a wynnowinge sheet & 4 sh...   10s
The wood in the barton worth   30s
Of wheat sowen 3 akers & barley sowen syx akers   £12
3 duckes   12d
3 horses and a colt worth   £6
5 kyen worth   £12 10s
10 green cheeses, 4 pounds of butter and 2 flytches of bacon   22s
Dettes dewe unto hym
Of Cetephyn Tritt   20s
Of John Prangnell   8s
Of Thomas Aldrydge   3s 4d
Of .... Bartram, wyddow   40d
Of Johan Goter, widow   9s
Of William Langrydge   6s
Of Thomas Prangnell   60s
Of Nycholas Ventham   ?d
                                                       Summa tot.   £120 15 8d

1691A/119   George Ventham, the elder, yeoman, of East Tytherley   1691

Inventory of ye goodes & chattells of George Ventham of East Tytherley
in ye county of South, yeoman.   December 1690.

Im primis   his wearing aparell   £3
In the two chambers within the hall
two fether beds with all sorts of beding belonging to them with one
testear bedstead & other lumber goods in these roms   £6

101

In ye chamber above staiers
one fether bed with the bedsteed & beding & other things ther   £5

In ye hall
two tabls with their frams, one forme, one great cuboard &
all other things in thatt rome   £1 10s

In ye buttery & ye two roms ajoyning to the buttery
the barells & all ye brewning vessel & bucketts & other wooden things
in these roms   £3
corn in ye barne of all sorts   £12 10s
the iron & laders about ye house   £1
one carte with whells (wheels) & one dung potte   £2
one plow & three harrows   £1 10s
five beast (livestock) small & great   £6
two fatte hoggs & three peggs   £5
two loads of hay   £2 10s
one mare   £4

In ye shope
2 hi... of board & all ye tolls (tools) ther   £2 10s
3 akers & five lugs of wheat on ye ground   £3 5s
money in ye house   £25
one great bible & other books   15s
the lease of ye living now in being as it is   £90

                                                       sum total   *£178 10s*

7
Manor Court Rolls

Over the centuries the feudal system on manor estates gradually became modified. By Tudor times the most common form of land tenure was copyhold, which had developed out of the old villein tenure, whereby a tenant had held his land in return for service to the lord of the manor on the demesne land. In the 16th century the service had generally been commuted into a regular rent, but copyholders still held their land through the manor courts and were still liable for such conditions as heriot and merchet payments. The tenant held a copy of the court rolls, or records of the court proceedings, and these acted as his title deeds, hence the name copyholder.

Many of the 16th and 17th century court rolls of the manor of East Tytherley and Lockerley have survived[1], and they give considerable insight into rural life in the villages at that time. The manor was granted to George Bainbridge by the king, Henry VII, in 1496. He had already been given the manor of Lockerley Butler in 1493, and from that time onwards the two manors were combined. However, they retained traces of their separate origins such as pasture rights on different areas of common land.

The manor courts were a combined Court Baron, Court Leet and View of Frankpledge and were held twice a year (see chap. 2). Freeholders and copyholders were obliged to attend and to pass judgement on the issues raised, an obligation known as suit of court. Tenants who defaulted, or failed to attend, and did not provide an essoin (a valid excuse and someone to attend by proxy) on three consecutive occasions, were fined for default. An official copy of the record of proceedings, was produced after a court had been held, which had to be written in Latin until 1733, except during the commonwealth period, 1649 - 1660[2]. The East Tytherley and Lockerley rolls of 1654 and 1655 are in English. Eighteen court rolls from between 1509 and 1681 were examined, chosen for the present work because they had survived in good condition and were reasonably legible rather than to get an even distribution over the time period. The rolls are given under their HRO reference numbers 5M58/1- 38.

The court roll always begins with a list of the homage, or jury, which were made up of twelve men who acted for all the tenants who owed suit of court. The list of names is of some interest in itself, since many of the surnames are of the families who lived for many centuries in the villages, Pragnell, Betteridge, Moore, Bonner and Ireland among others. The homage was then sworn in to make a true presentment. Attendance at manor courts appears to have been a tedious and time-consuming business, and both copyholders and freeholders were frequently named and fined for default of suit of court. Some prominent landholders from the surrounding countryside, including the Prior of Mottisfont, Lord Sandys, Thomas Welles and the Thistlethwaites of Norman Court, held land within the manor by freehold tenure, and were not infrequently among the defaulters. Presumably they did not find it difficult to pay the fine.

By the 16th century the tithing had come to mean an area within the manor, rather than simply ten households, and the manor of East Tytherley and Lockerley had three tithings, East Tytherley, Lockerley and Kimbridge, each with its own tithing man. The tithing man gave his report to the court, which included the relevant problems in his district and any changes in copyhold land tenure there.

Unfortunately the court rolls traditionally only included matters which involved finance in some way, such as the collection of money due, fines imposed for wrongdoing or changes in land holding. Much of the court discussion would have been concerned with the communal agriculture, reaching agreement about which crops to grow where, and when to allow grazing of the fallow. There would have been no benefit in having these decisions written down, since the people to whom they mattered were not literate and could not have read them. However, we can glean some information about farming practices, particularly the management of the common land used for grazing the farm animals. The manorial 'waste', or commons, included all the land which was not under cultivation as arable, managed as hay meadows or designated as prime pasture land. The manor parkland, although probably used for grazing, would have been treated separately. The common land included woodland and open areas of rough grazing, marsh and scrub. It is not possible to define precisely the areas which were used, but the court rolls do give an indication. In East Tytherley parish, there was the area known as Thornes (Fig. 5), which must have adjoined the present-day Thornes Wood. Thornes common stretched into Lockerley as far as Carter's Lake, but the grazing and pannage belonged to the East Tytherley copyhold tenants of the manor only. Carter's Lake was situated by the hamlet now called Carter's Clay. The East Tytherley commoners were allowed to cut bushes there, but not oak, ash, beech and elm saplings. They were not stinted, or restricted in the number of animals that they could graze at any one time, and they could drive the common to round up the animals by mutual agreement, rather than on set dates (5M58/31,38).

The waste from Carter's Lake to Cebell's Cross, together with the Green and Butler's Wood, were commons belonging to the Butler's tenants and they had rights of herbage, pannage, and cutting of furze, fern and bushes. Cebell's Cross was likely to have been the point on the Lockerley parish boundary in Newtown. Newtown is shown as Bell's Corner in the Enclosure Award map of 1815 (see chap. 9), and Bell's Cottage stands there today on the parish boundary. Both Carter and Cebell were local family names around Lockerley and East Tytherley; there was a Carter's Farm in Lockerley shown on an estate map in 1759[3], although not in the vicinity of Carter's Clay, and a George Kebill was recorded in the manor court rolls of 1509 (5M58/1). Both groups of tenants had rights of common from Queen Oak above Broughton to Bewlye (Bentley) Gate, and also to the Fower (four) Posts at Hampton Hill. In addition both groups intercommoned, or shared some common land, with Salisbury Cathedral, Lord Sandys, Sir Hugh Stubelye, Sir John Blackgrove and Mr Titchbourne. This included 8 acres of land which was later called Lockerley Green[4]. The tenants of both East Tytherley and Lockerley Butler had the right to take wood for stakes and well curbs, and could take ploughbote (wood for mending ploughs) and cartbote (wood for mending carts) if grown on their own holding (5M58/31,38).

Another reference to an area of common land, in the court roll of 1655 (5M58/31), states that the land called Common Plot between Hopcatch and Bentley Farm belonged to the lord of the manor of East Tytherley, and that the tenants had rights of common there. Both Hopcatch and Bentley still exist today as landmarks (Fig. 5).

Tenants had to pay for the right of pannage, and some of the court rolls include a list of pannage payments by villagers who had put their pigs into the woodland in the autumn when the acorns and beech mast had fallen onto the ground. The production of acorns on the oak trees is very variable and only about one year in three is a good mast year when an abundant crop is produced, but even in the absence of acorns the pigs could get a plentiful supply of extra food by rooting to dig up earthworms

Fig. 18 *Pigs foraging in woodland (AB)*

and the roots of plants. This fattened them up before the winter, when the breeding sows and young growing pigs were retained, while those which had reached pork or bacon weight were slaughtered. Although pigs could be slaughtered at any age, they did not reach bacon weight as early as they do today and would probably have been slaughtered at two years of age[5]. In Anglo-Saxon times pigs had been allowed into woodland from midsummer onwards, but the pannage had been progressively reduced over the following centuries and traditionally it had become a six week period from Michaelmas Day (Sept 29th). The lists of pannage payments give an indication of the scale of the local pig production, which was an important part of the diet at that time.

In 1509 (5M58/1) the following made payments for pannage for their pigs:

Richard Bonner	*5 pigs, 2 piglets*	*6d*
Marcus Woodford	*5 pigs*	*5d*
William Godwyn	*5 pigs*	*5d*
Richard Thomas	*9 pigs*	*9d*
Thomas Betrygge	*4 pigs, 2 piglets*	
Walter Moore	*6 pigs*	*6d*
Marcus Prangnell	*7 pigs, 2 piglets*	*8d*

Thomas Prangnell	11 pigs, 7 piglets	14 ½ d
Johanna Gaff	6 pigs	6d
William Hugman	2 pigs, 5 piglets	4 ½ d
John Ireland	8 pigs	8d
John Turnor	1 pig, 2 piglets	2d
John Lysset	4 pigs	4d

Inevitably the less scrupulous among the local population tried to avoid payment. In 1509, at the same time as the above pannage payments, Henry Botiller, the local miller, was fined 8d for having pigs illegally on Thornes, and 6d for putting his pigs on Ford Green (Ford Green was an area of common near Ford or Lockerley Mill). Randolf Lote had put four of his pigs onto Hodes Green (possibly the later Butts Green) and Critchells Green and was fined 4d.

Animals grazing the manorial waste would have been managed in very much the same way as animals on common land such as the New Forest are today. During the pannage season pigs were probably lured back home, or into an enclosure, at the end of the day with food. In that way they could have been controlled and not just disappeared into the landscape and become feral. Sheep, cattle and horses belonging to the manor tenants were allowed to graze certain areas of common land, the areas depending on whether where they lived had historically been part of East Tytherley or Lockerley Butler. They could turn animals out on the commons between the dates fixed by the custom of the manor only. Grazing would have been allowed during the summer months and although the dates are not known they were likely to have been similar to those for other nearby common land. The villagers of West Dean were allowed to use the common land on Dean Heath and Bentley Wood from May Holyrood (May 3rd) until St Martin's Day (Nov 11th)[6] and comparable dates were probably used in Tytherley and Lockerley.   The right to graze animals on common land was a very valuable one and determined how many animals a small farmer could keep. There was always the temptation to turn out a few extra animals onto an area where the owner did not have the right, or to let them graze there outside the official season. Henry Botiller, again in 1509, had depastured his sheep on Ford Green between the feast of St. Michael the Archangel (Sept. 29th) and the feast of St. Andrew (Nov. 30th) against the custom of the manor, and was fined 4d.

Not surprisingly the problem was an ongoing one; in 1648 and 1649 the manor courts were still dealing with very similar offences. Both Widow Busse and Widow Clifford had concealed the fact that they had no right to depasture their animals on Thornes, William Blake had put his sheep on the commons unlawfully and .... Goddard was to have his animals impounded as he repeatedly flouted the law (5M58/25,27,29). Illegally grazing animals were driven into the village pound when they could be caught, and the owner had to pay for their release. In 1648 Alexander Hinton broke into such an enclosure and took his animals away (5M58/25), for which he was fined 5s. A little later geese feeding on the commons were occupying the manor court's time. In 1662 Henry Case was not permitted to graze his geese in turns on Thornes (5M58/32) and ten years later Matthew Barlow MD (the doctor), Edward Spragg, and Thomas Pragnell had depastured their geese on the manorial waste against the custom of the manor (5M58/36) and were ordered not to graze either geese or cattle there in future.

In addition to unlawful grazing, stray animals appeared around the manor land from time to time, which was inevitable when animals were not kept in enclosed fields but grazed on common pasture under the eye of a shepherd or cowherd, or were turned onto common land. Stray animals were also held in the village pound and their owner, when identified, had to pay a fine for their return. In 1509 there was 1 stray sorrel (chestnut) horse in Lockerley in custody, 2 ewes with their lambs and a steer in Kimbridge, and 1 wether sheep in East Tytherley (5M58,1). There is no information about the methods of identification used locally in cattle, but they were probably branded. Most of the cattle and horses were likely to have been known individually and would not have posed too much of a problem, until they wandered rather further afield than usual. Sheep appear to have had ear tags or a tattoo mark. In 1545 a stray sheep had 'a half in one ear and a farthing (quarter) in the other', which were probably a form of ear tag (5M58/8). Another was 'marked' in both ears (5M58/20).

As well as dealing with aspects of farming, the manor court had a variety of complaints brought to their attention. One problem which seems to have been widespread in the 16th century was that of millers who 'took more than their due tolls'. From the Norman Conquest onwards, and probably before, the lord of the manor was legally able to compel his tenants to use his mill to have their corn ground, and to charge them for the privilege. It was an offence to take corn to be ground in a mill not belonging to the lord, or to grind it at home using a hand mill. The rate of multure, or the

Taking corn to the mill

fee for grinding, was assessed by volume, not weight and the miller used a measure to take an agreed proportion of the corn before it was ground. The rate of toll varied according to local custom and on the strength of the water-course driving the mill, for example 1/20th – 1/24th. These were the rates charged to customary tenants, free tenants paid less[7]. Since the toll was just a measure by volume taken out of the unground corn, it was relatively easy for an unscrupulous miller to take slightly more than he should have done out of everyone's sacks.

Fitzherbert in his Boke of Husbandry in 1523 had the following advice to housewives '*and to ordain corn and malt to the mill, and meete it to the mill, and from the mill, and see that thou have thy measure again beside the toll, or else the miller dealeth not truly with thee*'[8].

The millers in East Tytherley and Lockerley appear to have been just as corrupt as everywhere else. In 1509 the familiar Henry Botiller of Lockerley was fined 3d for taking more than his due of the mill tolls. Likewise Thomas Wyfold, miller of East Tytherley was fined 3d (5M58/1). In 1519 the offending millers were John Pynkernell and Robert Howchyn, who were both fined by the manor court (5M58/3). Henry Botiller also appeared before the manor courts for yet another of his sharp practices, when he brewed ale and 'broke the assize'. Where people sold beer or ale to other villagers it had to be of a certain standard strength, and similarly bread when sold had to be a certain weight; it was the 16th century equivalent of trades' description legislation. At the two courts held in April and October 1509 Henry Botiller and six others were variously fined for breaking the assize of ale (5M58/1). Keepers of alehouses had to have licences from the local justices, the conditions of which included not keeping open on the Sabbath, not permitting unlawful games, not harbouring wanderers and vagrants, nor infringing the regulations which established and maintained local respectability[9]. In 1665 John Wilkins, John Markman and Richard

Stock were accused of having sold beer without a licence, and having *'kept disorder in their houses by tippling on the Sabbath and at other times'* (5M58/31).

Whereas stray animals and people abusing the manorial grazing rights were the main problems arising out of the use of the common land of the manor of East Tytherley and Lockerley during the 16th century, encroachments were the main complaint on the manor court agenda in the mid 17th century. An encroachment was made when a person enclosed a piece of land to which he had no legal right, usually as a site for building a cottage. In an age when rural poverty was commonplace, erecting a hovel on a corner of common land was a relatively easy way to provide a home for the family. A small enclosure would give enough space to keep a few animals, which could then be grazed illegally on the commons, and there would be room to grow a few vegetables. During the second half of the 17th century there was a rapidly expanding population, which provided a considerable incentive to increasing agricultural productivity. Prices rose, especially grain prices, making the cost of living higher for the bottom end of society. The more energetic peasants acquired extra strips of arable land to till, raised

Fig. 19 *Peasant life. (T. Bewick)*

more animals, and became more affluent farmers. Their neighbours who had lost their land became landless wage labourers. There must also have been a few people who wanted something for nothing, or who enjoyed flouting authority, just as there are today. Encroachments were usually on the manorial common land, but at a time when boundaries were not drawn on a map, and were held to be where the oral tradition of the manor said that they had always been, it was hard to prove it when someone had pushed his garden boundary a few yards onto his neighbour's patch.

In 1648 seven people had made encroachments on the manorial waste in East Tytherley and six in Lockerley. In addition John Couse had enclosed a piece of the Green (Lockerley Green) to make a garden. Thomas Hacker had also made an encroachment in Lockerley; he had built a house and made fences round to form an orchard, which he had then planted with trees. He was fortunate, he was allowed to keep his enclosure, as was John Hatcher who was allowed to keep an encroachment on the common land provided that he paid 2s a year rent, and the back rent. The following year John Couse and the seven offenders in East Tytherley still had their encroachments, and the court ordered that they be demolished before the next court hearing. William Pearce, who had encroached onto the garden of Richard Kent, was also ordered to leave it before the next court (5M58/25,27). In 1655 six people, including two widows, had erected illegal cottages on Thornes and Carters Lake common land, and in Lockerley eight cottages had been erected in Butlers Wood. The problem was becoming more acute, and the court made the pronouncement that if cottages were erected illegally on the commons in either East Tytherley or Lockerley the manor tenants and freeholders were to assist in pulling them down (5M58/31).

However, the problem of encroachments did not go away. In 1670 Peter Good had made an encroachment on the waste at his home in Lockerley Street, with fences and hedges blocking the road, 'to the serious inconvenience of all the local people'. The manor court had a series of complaints about Peter Good, who had thrown stones onto the road in Lockerley Street which had also diverted a water channel, and he had not dug out the water course from Aldermoor as far as the flood hatch at Holbury Mill Bridge (5M58/35). Three years later he had not removed his enclosure, which he was using as a garden at his house, and the stones were still in a heap in Lockerley Street (5M58/36). The authority of the manor court to deal with people who persisted in flouting the rules appears to have been very limited.

The tenants who held common rights were obviously disadvantaged by the gradual erosion of the common grazing, but even pulling down some of the makeshift, hastily-erected huts and cottages could not turn back the tide. An estate map of the manor of Lockerley, made for Denys Rolle in 1759[3], shows thirteen cottages scattered around the edge of Butler's Wood common land. In 1797 Solomon Southrell paid his rent, but not the extra rent which he had agreed to pay for an encroachment on the Green made 6-7 years previously[10].

The manor courts also dealt with repairs around the manor holdings and the villages, principally making the decisions about what was necessary and who was responsible for carrying it out. Major repairs to bridges and village facilities were either carried out by the lord of the manor, or the lord supplied the timber, and the tenants carried out the work. In 1648 the park pale and boundary posts were in a poor state and a bridge was dangerous, all of which were to be repaired by the lord of the manor. The East Tytherley churchyard rails were also in a bad state, but they were to be repaired by the tenants (5M58/27). In 1655 South Bridge by Ford (Lockerley) Mill was to be repaired by the lord, as was Inn Bridge which was in poor repair at the south end and therefore the responsibility of East Tytherley manor (5M58/31). Inn Bridge therefore must have been at a crossing point on the river at the boundary of two manors, and on a road where there could have been an inn, and Kimbridge would seem the most likely location. The lord of the manor was also to find replacement timber for the pound in Lockerley which was in poor repair and the tenants were to carry out the renovation. It was agreed that a pair of stocks needed to be constructed in the tithing of East Tytherley (5M58/31), but unfortunately the court rolls make no comment as to why.

Repairs to individual properties also had to be considered by the courts and these were the responsibility of the tenants concerned, who sometimes needed a certain amount of coercion. In 1648 John Puncherton, gent, was ordered to repair his granary (5M58/27), showing that it was not just the poorer tenants who failed to carry out repairs. In 1655 the house of Nicholas Woodford needed new roof timbers which he was ordered to repair (5M58/31). Seven years later the aforementioned Nicholas Woodford and three others had not repaired their houses adequately, and in 1663 Woodford and two of the others still had not complied with the court orders (5M58/32). The only person who had, Augustine Russon, was in trouble again in 1670 over house repairs, which suggests that he had made a rather inadequate temporary job of it. He was sworn in as tithing man for East Tytherley the same year, so he was a reasonably respected member of society (5M58/35).

An important part of repair work was the clearing out of waterways and ditches. This was essential where the land was naturally poorly drained clay soil, or where water collected at the lowest point from the surrounding hills. The river Dun itself also needed to be kept in a clear-flowing channel to prevent it forming swampy areas, with the water just trickling diffusely through it. In 1655 the ditch from Carter's Lake was to be scoured by the local tenants (5M58/31). The ditch is a deep one which at that time probably held a significant volume of water. It runs alongside the present-day Lockerley to Romsey road for part of its course and if choked with debris, branches or vegetation would have flooded the road. In 1670 the water course needed to be dug out at Aldermoor, on the river upstream of Holbury Mill (5M58/35); Peter Good was supposed to have cleared it out, but had failed to do so. At the next court session Walter Thomas was instructed to cut the vegetation so that the water could return to its correct course.

Changes in tenancy among the copyholders were another regular part of the manor court sittings. Copyholders held their land from the lord of the manor through the manor court, and when they died or gave up their holding, their tenancy reverted to the lord. Copyhold tenure was often for three named lives so that the next named person then took the holding, agreeing at the court session to pay the heriot due to the lord, and to abide by the customs of the manor. A heriot was the best beast in the deceased's ownership. In 1519 Johanna Peke, widow, was granted the land which was formerly her husband's, and paid 2 capons (5M58/3). In 1670 (5M58/35) the various heriots falling due included 1 gelding, 1 cow, 1 horse and 1 capon.

Although the manor Court Leet had originally held local responsibility for law and order, which was devolved from the Crown, during Tudor times this was taken over by local Justices of the Peace who met formally four times a year at the quarter sessions. There they dealt with such problems as poor relief, licensing of ale houses, unlawful gaming and a variety of other matters. Under the Tudor reorganisation of local law and order the parish came to replace the tithing as the unit of local government, with much of the responsibility falling on the churchwarden. From that time onwards parishes became much more than ecclesiastical areas. In many cases the manor estate and the parish coincided, but this was not always so as the parishes in the Dun Valley did not correspond exactly with the various manors. The East Tytherley and Lockerley manor courts changed their emphasis during the 16th century and dealt with what was relevant to management of the manor estate. Persons who sold beer below the assize and similar offences were then dealt with at the quarter sessions. The gradual disintegration of the open field system by enclosure, with the resulting reduction in the areas of common land meant that communal agricultural decisions became less necessary, so that by the 18th century the manor courts ceased to have any function other than arranging estate tenancies.

8
The Accounts of Augustine Stevens

The estate accounts for 1680 for the manor of East Tytherley, which were prepared by the bailiff, Augustine Stevens, have survived intact, and present an interesting snapshot of life on a manor estate in the Dun Valley at that time[1]. It is only a snapshot, because although it gives a wealth of detail it is for one year only, and there was bound to be some annual variation. However, much will be typical and when it is added to the information from other sources it is a valuable document. The accounts were prepared for the lord of the manor, Sir Francis Rolle.

Fig. 20 *The accounts of Augustine Stevens, bailiff of East Tytherley manor, 1680. HRO ref. 9M60/6 (AB)*

In medieval times farming was very much a subsistence economy; a manor estate and all its tenants were primarily concerned with growing and rearing just sufficient food and other commodities such as wood, wool and leather to provide for their own requirements. During the 17th century farming was gradually moving much further towards a market economy. This was brought about because of a sustained growth in the population, particularly in the towns, and if they were to be fed farms needed to produce a surplus, particularly of corn. However, much of the production was still to meet local requirements and most estates were made up of mixed farms, but with regional differences in the degree to which they concentrated on corn or livestock[2]. The Dun Valley, with its varied soil types and fairly heavy woodland cover, was different from the open downland further north, and the East Tytherley manor accounts reflect this difference.

The accounts show what was present on the farm at the two important dates in the farming calendar, March 25th (Lady Day) at the end of the winter, and September 29th (Michaelmas Day) at the end of the summer production and harvest. They also show what had been sold, what had been bought in and what had been spent on production. The household accounts are included as well as they were an integral part of the estate economy.

Farm Animals in stock March 25th 1680:
14 cows, 10 heifers, 8 steers, 1 bull, 6 oxen and 14 calves, 681 sheep and 17 pigs.

In stock September 29th 1680:
24 cows, 12 steers, 2 bulls, 8 oxen and 10 calves, 748 sheep and 34 pigs.

Deaths March 25th – September 29th:
1 heifer, 5 adult sheep, 7 lambs and no pigs.

Slaughtered in house March 25th – September 29th:
34 sheep and 13 lambs.

Animals purchased:
6 cows, 2 steers and 1 bull.

Animals sold:
1 home-bred cow which fetched £4 10s and 40 ewes which were sold for £12 10s.

The cattle were a small herd presumably kept to provide butter and cheese for the manor house, and to provide working oxen. Although in general cart horses had taken over most of the farm work by this time, oxen would have been more useful on the heavy ground around East Tytherley, particularly for ploughing and hauling timber. There were no records of any of the dairy produce being sold, and as only one cow and no steers or heifers were sold, the herd was not kept to produce meat. There was no local breed of cattle in Wiltshire or Hampshire, so the herd was probably of rather mixed appearance. They were likely to have been bred on the farm as the cow which was sold was entered in the accounts as:

Received for one cow of your own breed the summe of   £4 10s.

Shearing sheep

A rather bigger enterprise was the sheep flock, although the numbers of animals were not very great when compared with the big downland flocks on Salisbury Plain and the Hampshire Downs. East Tytherley is very much on the edge of the downland, and the large areas of heavy ill-drained clay soil around parts of the estate were not very suitable for sheep, particularly before modern field drainage. The East Tytherley sheep were probably mainly kept to produce wool which was sold, providing a reasonable profit for the estate. There was little emphasis on meat production, although some of the 40 ewes sold could have been used for meat. On the chalk downlands of Wiltshire and Hampshire sheep were kept principally to provide manure for the arable land; during the daytime they grazed on the downland pasture, and were then driven back to the arable fields where they spent the night confined in pens, a practice known as the sheepfold. The hurdle pens were moved along every night so that all parts of the field were fertilised. This was carried out on a huge scale in downland areas, with very large flocks providing manure to fertilise the poor thin chalk soil so that it could produce good crops of corn. In East Tytherley, which is only partly on the chalk, the practice is likely to have been carried out to a much lesser extent. The sheep would have been the local horned breed, the old Wiltshire Horn, or the Hampshire equivalent which was very similar. The Wiltshire Horn was a strong-bodied long-legged sheep, adapted to walking long distances from the sheep-fold to the downs on a daily basis. The fleece was fairly light, but the wool was moderately fine and was used for making the local broad cloth[3].

Sales Wool sales £47 9s 10d, 40 ewes sold £12 10s, Skins of sheep and lambs killed or died £1 12s 8d, Tallow 13s 3d.
Total sales **£62 11s 5d.**

Expenses Cost of washing and shearing the sheep £27 5s, Sheep hurdles £5 4s, Sheep pens at Wherwell Fair 4s 4d.
Total expenses **£32 13s 4d.**

The numbers of deaths among the sheep and lambs was very low, but it did not include the winter months. It also suggests that the lambing period was probably complete, or nearly so, by Lady Day, as that would have been the time of greatest loss. Many of the 34 sheep which were killed in house may have had either acute or chronic disease problems, been injured, or had lambing difficulties; such animals would have been killed while they could still provide a usable carcase. There would also have been old sheep in poor condition, which were not fit enough to be driven to Weyhill or other sheep fairs. The skins from both the slaughtered animals and those which had died were sold, the fat was rendered down for tallow and much of the meat would have been edible. The lambs which were killed were probably intended for meat for the house.

There is no detailed information about the pigs but it is likely that a small nucleus of breeding animals was kept to provide pigs to rear for pork and bacon.

The arable crops grown on the estate arable land that year were wheat and barley, while peas, oats and hop clover were also grown to provide animal food. The principal cereal crop was wheat, a fair proportion of which was sold in batches at various times during the year. In March 1680 the amount left in stock from the previous year was 5 bushels. One hundred and ninety six bushels of old wheat from last year's harvest and 36 bushels of the new wheat, were sold '*to several persons at several times*' during the period March 25th and September 29th, raising the sum of £39 8s 5d in total. The price per bushel varied from 3s to 3s 6d for old wheat and 3s 8d to 4s for the new wheat. In addition, 82 bushels of wheat were used 'in the house' during the time period, leaving 27 ½ bushels in stock at the end of September. However, all the quantities of corn, both wheat and barley, given in the accounts are the amounts of threshed corn, they do not include stocks of unthreshed corn in the barn. Threshing with flails, followed by winnowing, was carried out over a prolonged time, and during 1680 large amounts of the previous year's corn was still being threshed. This makes it difficult to work out the quantity harvested in that year.

Forty-five bushels of old barley was sold at 1s 11d to 1s 6d per bushel over the time period March to September, producing a total of £4 4s 2d. Two hundred and twenty-five bushels of the old barley was used as seed corn to produce the next crop, and 93 bushels were used on the farm. Although some of the best barley may have been used for malting, the poorer quality grain would have been animal feed. Fifty-nine acres of the new crop were sown in the spring. Some seed barley for this was also purchased, 56 bushels costing £5 7s 4d. Large amounts of malt were also bought in, 296 bushels were purchased at a cost of £29 8s 8d, and the quantity used in the house was 237 bushels. Hops were grown on a small scale, but none were sold, although by the late 17th century they had become

Threshing corn

a commercially viable crop. Presumably the home-grown hops were to be added to the 237 bushels of malt for the mansion house beer.

Oats, peas and clover were also used for animal feed. The oats were principally used to feed the horses, which had consumed 569 bushels at the end of the time period. Thirty-one acres of oats were grown on the farm in 1680 and large quantities were also bought in. A small area (9 acres) of home-grown peas was cut that year, and one bushel was purchased, and 80 bushels of hop clover seed was bought for sowing.

During the 17th century agricultural improvements were taking place which meant that leaving the ground fallow every third year was no longer essential for the production of good harvests of cereal crops. The addition of chalk or lime as a dressing on all but the naturally very chalky arable ground had been introduced a century earlier, and had become commonplace by 1680. Augustine Stevens's accounts include payment for a total of 29 quarters of lime, large amounts of which would have gone on the land. Other uses for it would have been for mortar, plaster and limewash for building renovation and repair. A more recent agricultural improvement was the introduction of new fodder crops in the mid 17th century. East Tytherley, along with many other areas, was by this time using crops such as peas and clover, which fixed atmospheric nitrogen in the soil, thereby improving its subsequent fertility. By changing the crop rotation to include clover and ryegrass hay after two seasons of arable crops, a fallow year could be avoided. Hop clover (*hop trefoil*) as specified in the accounts, was better on the higher ground than broad clover, which did better on the valley soils[4]. A crop which was conspicuous by its absence in the accounts was turnips, which were introduced as winter feed for cattle and sheep during the 17th century and were gaining popularity in both Hampshire and Wiltshire at that time[5,6]. Turnips, or turneps as they were called, were very difficult to fit into an open field rotation, which may have been why they were not used locally in 1680.

Against the profits of sales there were a number of expenses incurred, from ploughing the land to threshing the crop following harvest, and transporting corn to the local markets.

Payment of carters and ploughmen   £14 4s 11d

Hire of plough teams
Hugh Wilton for 2 days with his team at barley sowing   12s
Robert Downe for 3 days the same season   12s

Mowing of barley
Robert Cole for mowing 6 acres in the Pick and Redhill   5s
Nicholas Woodford for mowing Garrels   10d

Oats
Nicholas Kingman for mowing 14 ½ acres at Costards   12s 1d

Peas
John Fabian for cutting 9 acres in the Vicaridge Field   18s
Seven extra men were employed for one month at harvest, the Months Men.

Threshing
Edward Luke was paid for threshing 262 bushels of wheat   £2 14s 7d
Anne Plumley was paid for winnowing 32 quarters and 6 bushels 2s 9d

William Bedford was paid for threshing 94 bushels of barley   7s 10d
Anne Plumley was paid for winnowing 10 quarters and 6 bushels   11d

<u>Portage of Corn</u>
Paid for carrying sacks of corn to Sarum and other markets   6s

Winnowing: separating out the grain

The field names for the mowing of the barley are of interest in that they suggest that the demesne arable was no longer in the common fields, and also that they were in the area of the later Queenwood Farm, on the lighter chalk soil. Queenwood had been enclosed by 1708 and at that time included:

A close of arable called Vicaridge Field (32 acres) and fields called Red Hills/Rodd Hill and Peeke (Pick)[7].

Although the estate woodland did not produce an annual crop like the arable land, nevertheless the sale of coppiced underwood was a valuable source of income. Timber trees were a very long-term investment, oak for timber was usually cut after about 70 years' growth, but the hazel underwood which grew among the timber trees was cut at much more frequent intervals. Hazel for sheep hurdles was cut at around 7 years' growth, and when the various coppices were cut in different years there would have been a coppice due for cutting most years. In the autumn the standing coppice was sold in lots for cutting during the winter months. Thirteen acres of underwood was sold in Laine Coppice in 1680 for **£61 18s**. Unlike the production of cereal crops, which involved ploughing, sowing, weeding, harvesting and threshing there was very little annual expenditure needed in producing an area of hazel coppice. The wood bank, usually with a ditch outside, required some maintenance, and the hedge on top needed to be cut and laid from time to time to make the coppice animal-proof when the newly-cut coppice stools were growing up. Some hazel was required on the estate, and payments were made for cutting this, and making some of it up into the bundles or faggots used in bread ovens or kilns. The hurdle maker, John Phillips, was paid for making 4 dozen hurdles.

Another source of income was the agistment of horses. Large numbers of horses, mainly yearlings too young to be broken in and worked, were grazed during the summer months at Holbury. Their owners paid 6d to 8d a week per horse for them to graze for variable periods of time, up to five months.

One expense recorded in the accounts was payment for hedging, which is of interest as it probably indicates that some of the fields had been enclosed, and that quickthorn, or hawthorn, hedges were being planted. Walter Goeter was paid for *'shearing all the hedges'*, a term which they were unlikely to have used for laying hedges in the traditional way, but cutting the newly-planted hawthorn hedges must have looked very like shearing sheep. Payments were also made for *'making hedges'* in Vicaridge Field, Lower Park and other places. This was likely to have meant planting hawthorn hedges in fields which were previously open fields. Enclosure of the East Tytherley manor estate was happening around this time, and because much of it took place informally by local agreement rather than by parliamentary acts of enclosure, there are few written records about how and when it occurred. Indications such as field names and terms like 'shearing hedges' are a useful guide.

One annual source of income to Sir Francis Rolle was the receipt of the tithes of the parish, which in this case belonged to him, as lord of the manor, rather than the rector (see chap. 5). The amount that he received during the period March – September 1680 amounted to **£43 15s 9d,** as the tithes had been commuted from payments in kind to an equivalent payment in money. In addition there was **£6 5s** from the tenement of a deceased member of the parish, which was made up from the value of three loads of hay plus payments from people who had grazed animals on the property since his death. This seems to be a considerable sum to add to the accounts, but when the parson did not receive the tithes, he had to be paid. Mr. John Hilary received a salary of £10 a quarter, so £10 was debited from the accounts in May and August.

The servants' wages for half a year also had to be paid out. Nineteen servants were paid a total of 46 12s, most of whom received between £1 and £4, except Augustine Stevens himself, who had £7. There were also bills to be paid:

Killing Moles
Paid William Terry for killing moles from our Lady Day last past to this day   *£1 3s*

Coles Bought
Paid George Fussard of Southampton for 508 bushells of seacoales att 9s the bushel £19 1s (seacoal was ordinary coal as opposed to charcoal).

Paid Edward Damerham for 301 sacks of charcoals att 10d a sack with
carriage   £12 18s 10d

Bricklayers Work
Paid Thomas Philpes for work done by him   £5 17s 10d
Paid Thomas Sturgis and others for work by them done by the day
                                                        £1 15s 10d

Smith's Worke
Paid Silvester Langridge att Gilhame for work by him made and done
between 25 March and 29 Sept   £19 15s 2d

Carpenters etc
Paid William Skilton and others for work done in the said time   £4 1s 6d
Paid the same for sawing of square timber and board att 3s and 2s 6d the
hundred   £1 13s 6d

Wheelers Worke
Paid Thomas Russell   £1 11s 2d
Paid the same   12s 2d

Coopers Work
Paid Richard Colbarne   £3 5s

Collarmakers Work
Paid Nicholas Hall for work done by him   £1 14s 10d
(for making or repairing horse collars)

Carriage of Goods

Eleven people were paid for transporting coal from Redbridge (near
Southampton) on separate occasions, the coal having been taken there by sea.
The general expenses of the household were also included in the accounts,
which make interesting reading and they are therefore reproduced below
just as they were written.

Expences in Houskeeping
Paid for severall things for and towards housekeeping between 25th
March and 29th Sept   £105 19s 2d
Paid for stowring sand   2s
Paid for bringing a letter from Sarum   1s 6d

*Paid a messenger that brought tidings of the death of John Thistlethwaite
of Winterslow* 1s

Paid for broomes 2s 11d

Paid Thomas Jeames for fetching of water from Bambridge welle 5s 6d

Paid for 18 pairs of childrens gloves 8s

Paid for a basket of Row for Mrs Bull 6d

Paid Mr Courtney for paper, wax and quills 8s 6d

Paid for a bushell of beanes 5s

Paid for a paire of scissrs 6d

Paid for sieves and mending of sieves 2s 2d

Paid Thomas Hatcher for carrying of things to Hampton (Southampton) 1s

Paid for 16 bushells of salt att 2s a bushel £1 6s 8d

Paid for sand 1s

Paid for 4 quire of guilded paper 2s

Paid Thomas Downes for mendingsackes 10d

Paid for 3 dozen of quart bottles 7s 6d

Paid Goody Williams for honey 1s 1d

Paid for row for Mrs Bull 6d

Paid for broomes 2s 8d

Paid Mrs Dobbs for leaches 2s 6d

Paid goodman Burret for mending the malt mill 3s

*Paid Richard Bonner for his halfe years clerkes wages and ending at
Easter last past* 4s

Paid Richard Mearsh for 7 grosse of tobacca pipes (clay pipes) 10s 6d

Paid for sand 4s

Paid for broomes 3s 4d

Paid Thomas Downes wife for spinning of lambs woole 2s

Paid for books that Mr Hilary bought at Sarum 1s 4d

Paid to John Chauntrell's daughter for peares 6d

Paid for a mat to lay att the parlour door 3s

Paid for a chatechir (catechism) *book* 3d

Paid for announce (an ounce) *of white sewing silke* 1s 6d

Paid for nails for the coach 6d

Paid for 30 bushells of salt att 16d the bushel £2

Paid for mopps 1s 6d

Paid for sand 8d

Paid for broomes 1s 6d

Paid goodman Row for taking oping Mr Staffe 1s

Paid for thread 3d

Pd for salt stones 5s

Pd for broomes   1s 6d

Pd for crying 2 steares in Romsey that were newly bought and strayed
away   4d

Pd Richard Mongey for looking to the swans and for yeares salary due   17s

Pd for 24 broomes   1s 6d

Pd Richard Mearsh for 9 grosse of tobacco pipes att 18d a grosse 13s 6d

Pd James Spragg for grinding 26 bushell of mault att 1d a bushel   2s 2d

Gave to Mr Rolles maid   1s

Paid for paper and ink   3s 4d

Paid for 2 tubbs and kiver (barrels) *att Weighill*   £2 12s

Paid for shreds of hatt pareings for the gardiner   7s 1d

Paid for sweeping chimneys   2s 6d

Paid goody Downes for spinning lambes   1s 9d

Paid for horse hire for Mr Watte   1s 6d

Paid for a silk lace   4d

Gave att Sarum when the children were there   2s

Paid for gloves for the children   3s 6d

Paid for 6 paires of gloves for monethesmen (months men at harvest)   6s

Paid for rakes and forks for haying and harvest   7s 9d

Payments were also made to the warrener for rabbits, the ironmonger, the
pewterer and others.

The accounts of Augustine Stevens show how East Tytherley manor was
organised in 1680, when many, if not most, of the local villagers were
involved with the manor in some way. Large numbers of people were
employed for at least part of the year, since both agriculture and housework
were very labour-intensive. There were 19 regular employees, and very
many more people who were paid for carrying out specific tasks, or were
taken on just for the harvest. The accounts also give an insight into what
the countryside would have looked like, and the payment of tradesmen and
craftsmen shows the variety of activities which were taking place there.

9
Changes in the Countryside

The 17th century was the beginning of a period of significant change in the Hampshire and Wiltshire countryside, mainly due to the developments in agriculture which were happening at that time. Industrialisation was still two centuries away, but many improvements were taking place which allowed greater production and efficiency. New crops were being introduced, there was more emphasis on putting fertilizers on the fields, land was being drained more effectively and water meadows were being created in the river valleys. Many of the agricultural improvements were seen to be much easier to implement where the land was enclosed, and under the direct control of the farmer in charge of it. Changes could be brought about in the open arable fields and communal grazing, but it had to be by the consent and cooperation of the landlord and all of the tenants, an individual farmer could not try out a new idea. These were the sentiments behind the drive towards enclosure as being the way forward for agriculture, which had been an ongoing controversy throughout the previous century.

Enclosure

There were two forms of enclosure which were under debate, one of which was the bringing into cultivation of the manorial waste, those areas of the manor estate which were rough grazing land or woodland. The other was the reorganisation of the open field system so that everyone had their arable land in one block rather than in scattered strips, and the distribution of the areas of common grazing among those who had held the right to depasture animals there. People were allocated land in proportion to their original holding, and in return they renounced all their previously-held common rights. The advantages of enclosure were undeniable, but there were serious drawbacks. The open field system supported many more people than when the same area was enclosed, and those who had most to lose were the cottagers and smallholders. The land which they were allotted would not support many animals when compared with grazing on large areas of common land. Landlords usually favoured the changes, and it was very hard for smallholders to oppose them. Many became landless labourers, and their holdings were taken over by other tenants, who held larger, more viable farm units. There were also some advantages in having scattered strips of arable land, as it reduced the chances of losing the whole crop to disease, pests or the weather. The arguments continued throughout the 17th and 18th centuries, and the move towards enclosure proceeded at different rates in different parts of the country. Most of the chalk downland areas of Wiltshire remained unenclosed during the 17th century, whereas in the dairy-farming regions of north and west Wiltshire there had been considerable enclosure during the 16th century[1]. Similar conditions applied in Hampshire, where enclosure was gradually taking place by various informal and formal means[2]. The enclosure of a manor estate could happen in a variety of ways, and many of the earlier enclosures were by informal mutual agreement. It was comparatively easy for a landlord who owned all the land in the parish to change the system by altering the arrangement of the land when tenancies fell due. There is no written record where this has happened, but tenancy agreements, where they are available, may indicate for example that a holding still has common rights. There are also records of disputes about villagers' rights which indicate that they still existed.

In 1682 an indenture was drawn up between Sir John Evelyn, lord of the manor of West Dean, and Henry Whitehead of Norman Court, West Tytherley[3], which terminated a long-standing disagreement about common rights on Frenchmoor Common, also called Tytherley Common. Evelyn granted to Henry Whitehead, to William Hussey, the parson of West Tytherley, and to the tenants of that manor the right of common of pasture on Frenchmoor Common, without *let, trouble, disturbance or molestation by the inhabitants of Frenchmoor*, At that time Frenchmoor was a detachment of Broughton, and the inhabitants were therefore tenants of John Evelyn, who owned Broughton manor in addition to West Dean. They presumably considered that only they had the pasture rights on Frenchmoor Common.

In 1692 an indenture for a messuage in East Dean called Brocknes included common of pasture[4], whereas another lease in East Dean in 1716, this time for a cottage and half an acre of garden and orchard[5], makes no mention of common rights, but does include the requirement to work for the landlord at reaping for one day at harvest.

A map of the manor of Lockerley belonging to Denys Rolle, lord of the manors of East Tytherley and Lockerley, dated 1759 shows part of the estate divided up into separate farms, but 286 acres of land around Butler's Wood was still common[6]. Three other small areas of common land also remained, Critchell's, Butts and Lockerley Greens, which have never been enclosed and remain as common land to this day. Unfortunately there is little information about East Tytherley parish, since only a very limited tithe map was produced; the field names on tithe maps are often strong indicators of how the land had been used in earlier times. Augustine Stevens's accounts suggest that the demesne farm of East Tytherley manor had probably already been enclosed by 1680.

A survey of the manor in East Dean and Lockerley belonging to the Dean and Chapter of Salisbury Cathedral[7] in 1797 makes it clear that most of the estate land was still very much part of the old system, but was gradually moving towards enclosure. One of the tenants has many small lots of ½ to 3 acres listed as being in the common fields of East Dean, together with common of pasture for 50 sheep on the Down. This holding is a typical yardland (see chap. 2) of 27 acres with arable land spread around the four common fields, called Hill Field, Lower Field, Middle Field and West Field. However, two of the Cathedral's other holdings of a similar size show moves to consolidate the strips into larger blocks. One (26 acres) has part of the land in closes, or enclosed fields, but also has 2 acres split into 3 lots in Hill common field, and one lot in East Dean common meadow. The other (23 acres) has all the land in closes, and there is no mention of the common fields, or of common rights. The Green in Lockerley is described as '8 acres of common ground'. The estate tenants appear to have intercommoned on The Green with other local inhabitants, and the Dean and Chapter were obviously considering enclosure as a good economic move:

'Various occupiers of land and others in Lockerley turn their cattle upon it, but by the account of Aaron Edwards, a very ancient inhabitant of Lockerley, it was formerly depastured by the tenants of the Dean and Chapter only. It is of little value but may be turned to account by portioning it among the respective tenants, permitting them to convert it to arable, for which they ought to pay additional rent.'

Enclosure by formal agreement was another way of approaching the problem, and provided a legally-binding agreement with the paperwork to prove it. In 1755 the tenants of the manor of East Tytherley surrendered their common rights in Thornes Wood or Common to Denys Rolle, lord of the manor of East Tytherley[8]. Six named tenants surrendered *'their interest and rights of common, right of feed, common of pasture and other profits and advantages, and any claim in law.'* Denys Rolle purchased the rights for £54 17s 2d.

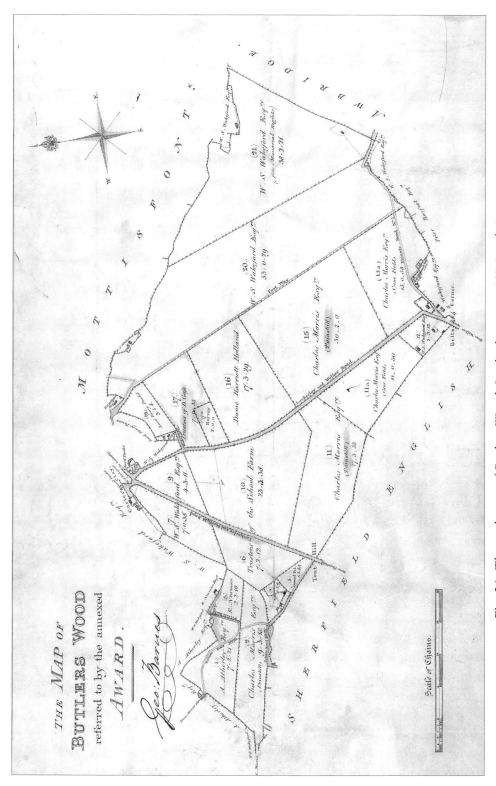

Fig. 21 *The enclosure of Butlers Wood, Lockerley, 1815. HRO ref. Q23/2/78*

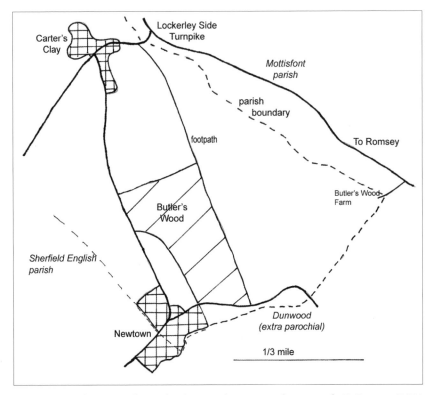

Fig. 22 *Butlers Wood, Lockerley, as shown on the 1st. ed. O.S.map.(MB)*

Where agreement could not be reached among the parties concerned, enclosure by a parliamentary Act was resorted to. Parliamentary enclosure began in Hampshire in 1709 and continued until 1888[9]. No parts of either East Dean or East Tytherley parishes were enclosed in this way, but some parts of Lockerley were. In 1815 there was an Act of Parliament for the enclosure of Butler's Wood[10]. In addition to the large allotments allocated to the major landholders there were some small ones to cottagers of a few acres. Even smaller were the allotments made to people who had 'encroached within 20 years of the time of enclosing', which were less than an acre in extent and would only have provided a large kitchen garden. These illegal encroachments on the common land, where the owners had managed to scratch a living by use of the commons, would now have become scarcely viable. The map produced in 1815 accompanying the enclosure award (Fig. 21) shows several cottages around Bell's Corner, which was situated at the far end of the former common land and adjoining the parish boundary, and there are also a few cottages shown around Carter's Clay. These are likely to be the twelve encroachments which gained legalised allotments at enclosure. In the Lockerley tithe map of 1840 an increased number of dwellings is shown in both these areas, and by 1871 considerably more houses appear on the first edition Ordnance Survey map, particularly around Bell's Corner which had become a distinct hamlet, and was now called Newtown (Fig. 22).

The Swing Riots

Throughout much of Britain enclosure of the common arable fields and the manorial waste had an enormous impact on the lives of the rural population. Hitherto agricultural labourers had managed to support their families just above the poverty line because the wages they had received for general farm work had been significantly augmented by their common rights. They could graze a few animals, cut fern for animal bedding, take fallen wood for fuel, and the corn gleaned in the stubble fields after harvest by their wives and children was often equivalent to the wages for a few weeks' work as a labourer. At enclosure villagers were granted allotments in lieu of common rights and strips in the common arable fields, but this did not compensate for the loss of the traditional way of life. The problem would have been minimised if wages had increased and paid employment been easily available, but wages fell with respect to prices at the end of the 18th century. Conditions varied during the early part of the 19th century; there were external forces such as war with France, which made corn growing profitable and helped the rural economy, unfortunately balanced by poor weather conditions shortly after the war had ended, which resulted in high prices and increased unemployment. In 1816 this led to civil unrest and rioting, particularly in the eastern counties[11].

Difficulties such as these were part of the wider problems of poverty, particularly among the lower end of society, which are discussed in Chapter 10, but in the countryside they were made worse by what the agricultural workers perceived as creeping industrialisation, and the increasing use of threshing machines became a major cause of conflict. Threshing machines had been introduced during the Napoleonic war as a valuable aid when there was a labour shortage, but in the 1820s they were seen as supplanting the traditional winter occupation for labourers in cereal-growing areas. Hand threshing with flails provided work for about three months when other work was scarce. The unrest erupted again in 1830, this time briefly and explosively in what became known as the Swing Riots, one of the worst-ever disturbances in rural England. Incendiarism and the breaking of machinery, particularly threshing machines, were widespread and there were also wage riots, threatening letters and robbery. Many of the letters which were sent to farmers were signed with the pseudonym 'Captain Swing'. The origin of the name is uncertain but one plausible theory is that the leaders of the harvest gangs, who were known as Captains, kept their men scything in unison as they moved across the field with the command 'altogether, swing'. Another theory is that it was derived from 'swingel', the name of the flexible part of the threshing flail[12]. Southern England was particularly badly affected by the riots, especially Hampshire and Wiltshire, where the movement really gained momentum. When the riots were over there were at least 300 prisoners in each of the two counties, compared with 160 in Berkshire and Buckinghamshire and about 100 in Kent.

There were many incidents in the area around the Dun Valley during late November 1830. One of the most notable riots was in Fordingbridge, south of Salisbury in the Avon Valley on November 23rd. The riot was led by James Thomas Cooper, a 33 year old ostler from East Grimstead, who rode a white horse and was styled 'Captain Hunt'. After burning threshing machines in the countryside all around, about 300 labourers marched into the town, demanded money and broke the machinery in two nearby mills, a sacking factory and a threshing machine factory. Cooper was arrested, tried, and was executed in Winchester on January 15th 1831. All the men condemned at the Special Commission, which had been set up in the worst affected counties to hold the trials, and those awaiting trial, were brought into the yard to watch the hanging. His body was taken back to his home village, East Grimstead, and buried in the old churchyard in West Dean. His gravestone stands in the graveyard there along with other family graves of that time[13,14].

On November 22nd a threshing machine in West Dean, the property of Joseph Whicher, was destroyed by a mob. Several of the men in the mob were recognized, but do not appear among the lists of those arrested or charged. On the same day, just over Dean Hill in Whiteparish, a mob of 100 people rioted and broke a threshing machine with a sledge hammer and an axe[15].

On November 23rd about 50 people collected in West Grimstead, and having destroyed a threshing machine, the property of Mr. Rumboll, they demanded straw so that they could burn it. Mr. Rumboll recognised some of the faces in the mob, which included those of Henry Herrington, William Rogers, William Luffman and Thomas Gange. The record of prisoners who

THE HOME OF THE RICK-BURNER.

Fig. 23 *Agricultural unrest. (J.Leech, in Punch,1844)*

were committed to Fisherton Gaol, Salisbury, on December 2nd included Henry Herrington, William Luffman and Thomas Gange, who were charged with having riotously assembled and broken a threshing machine. Their case was heard on January 3rd 1831 at the Special Commission of Assizes which had been hastily assembled in Salisbury at that time, and on January 4th they were sentenced to be transported to Australia for seven years[16]. There were also many other incidents throughout Wiltshire, all within the space of about two weeks.

Similar problems were also happening further down the Dun Valley. On November 22nd a large mob destroyed the turnpike gates at East Dean and East Tytherley. The following day the mob returned and ordered the toll collectors and their families to leave their houses saying that '*it is our intention to destroy all parsons, excise men and turnpikes in the country*'. The houses were then set on fire. William Southwell, aged 30, was tried at Winchester on January 4th with having riotously assembled in East Tytherley and destroyed the turnpike gate there. He was sentenced to imprisonment for three weeks in the House of Correction, with hard labour[17].

Another description of an incident which was happening at the same time is contained in an extract from a letter from East Tytherley dated November 22nd[18]:

This morning, about nine o'clock, we were alarmed by the appearance of a mob, which assembled at the door, and gradually increased to between two and three hundred men, who insisted on Webb and Aylward, two farmers, accompanying them. They appeared at Broughton and went to Mr. Tyrrell's, the curate of Lockerley, for money and paid their respects to us, as I have stated, this morning. From hence they went to Mottisfont to the Rev. Mr. St. John's, and we have heard that there was another assemblage on the Romsey road. Whilst here they insisted on our giving them twenty sovereigns, but Mr. Webb got them away by giving 8.

The riots and criminal acts only lasted for a few weeks, and those who had been charged and arrested did not have to wait long for retribution. The setting up of Special Commissions to try the prisoners followed swiftly, and although there was time for petitions to be lodged, to spare some of the prisoners and to reduce the sentences which they had received, the whole affair was over very quickly. A total of 1976 prisoners were tried in 34 counties, and following the commutation of many of the sentences, 19 were finally executed, 481 were transported to Australia and 644 received prison sentences. Of the rest 800 were acquitted or bound over to keep the peace[19]. Naturally, the problems of rural poverty and unemployment did not go away when the riots were over, and they are discussed further in Chapter 10. They also led to different sections of the general population trying to address the issues in a variety of ways, such as Robert Owen and the rise of his socialist movement, and they gave momentum to the nonconformist religious feeling that was becoming widespread in rural areas.

Water Meadows

One of the important developments in agriculture in the 17th century was the creation of water meadows along the valleys of rivers where the water had filtered through chalk. This involved the damming up of a river with a weir, and the channelling of the head of water which collected behind it onto the riverside meadows in a controlled fashion at strategic intervals. The water was diverted by opening hatches into carrier channels which then allowed a continuous sheet of water to spill over the ground, a process called drowning, and was afterwards collected up into drains and returned to the river some distance downstream of the weir. The procedure was carried out during the autumn and again at intervals after Christmas. The river water was always a few degrees above freezing, and provided it was kept flowing across the grass and did not remain static, it ensured that the ground was at a high enough temperature for the grass to grow in the early spring. The lime-rich water from chalk streams also encouraged a better mixture of grass strains to grow[20].

The production of good yields of corn relied on adequate sheep manure, which in turn depended on keeping as many sheep as the land would support, not only during the summer months but through the winter as well. By early spring the previous year's hay was finished, and the new grass had not started to grow, which restricted the number of sheep which could be kept. Water meadows allowed an earlier growth of grass than normal, which filled the 'hungry gap' and allowed a bigger flock to be maintained. By the time that the sheep had eaten down the water meadow other grass on the estate was beginning to grow, and the sheep could be moved onto that. The water meadows then produced a good crop of hay. Water meadows began in the early 17th century and by the 1660s had become an established feature on many chalkland manors[21]. There are the remains of water meadows along many stretches of the Avon and its tributaries in Wiltshire and further south where it flows through Hampshire, which have been described in detail by Cowan[22]. The Test and the Itchen in Hampshire also had extensive water meadows.

Against this background it is not surprising that the manors with land bordering the River Dun also wanted to develop water meadows. The damming of a river and construction of the water channels needed to drown an area of meadow changed the water flow of the river upstream, which was not a problem where only one landowner was involved, but

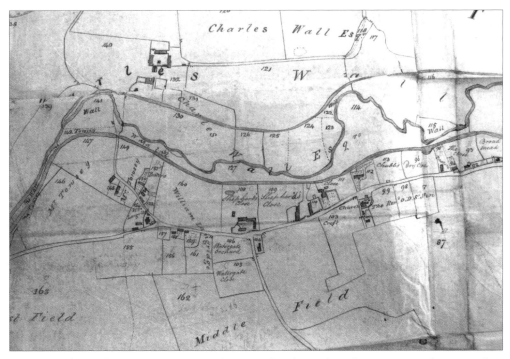

Fig. 24 *Map of East Dean c 1830, showing the channel to the water meadows north of the river and canal. WSHC ref. 776/394 (AB)*

liable to cause a dispute when a different manor was affected. In the 17th century the Whitheads of Norman Court, West Tytherley, owned a manor estate in East Dean, through which flowed the river Dun. By good fortune, or design, they also held a freehold property immediately upstream of this land, which was part of the manor of West Dean. Richard Whithead appears to have come to an agreement with Sir John Evelyn of West Dean, by which a weir was constructed on the freehold estate and a channel was cut to deliver water to the meadows bordering on the river in East Dean (Fig. 24). In return Evelyn and his tenants were to be allowed free access to any of the chalk pits in West Tytherley or elsewhere, as Evelyn wanted to turn an area of common land into arable, and needed chalk to improve the land while doing so. General ill-feeling seems to have developed between the two parties, finally resulting in a court case in *c* 1666[23]. By this date Richard Whithead was dead and the case involved his son Henry. Sir John Evelyn maintained that Richard Whithead had offered to compensate the tenants in West Dean who had land upstream of the weir, and on that basis the weir and channels had been allowed. While the newly-created water meadows had increased the value of the land for the Whiteheads by £50 a year, the West Dean tenants had not been compensated, and had been stopped from taking the chalk which they had been promised. Evelyn had threatened to dismantle the weir, but Richard Whithead's son, Henry, had offered that he would allow the extraction of chalk to continue when his father died, as he would then be in control. This had not happened, the tenants of West Dean upstream of the weir continued to complain, and the very frustrated Sir John Evelyn *'caused the boards of the said weare to be plucked up to keepe the said water in the current as formerly before the stopping and diversion by the weare sluice and new channel'*. The outcome of the dispute is not clear, but the timing of it must have run on into the next argument between Sir John Evelyn and Henry Whithead, over common rights as described above. The water meadows in East Dean were still referred to as such on the East Dean tithe map of 1839, and the remains of the water channels with their bridges and hatches can be seen today in the fields beside the river in East Dean downstream from Park Farm (Fig.XIX, p155).

Chalk

The argument over the supply of chalk does highlight the changes which were taking place on the commons of West Dean during the 17th century. Evelyn had *'grubbed upp neere one hundred acres of ground in West Deane aforesaid, being parte of the ancient waste of West Deane, with the intention to improve the same by chalke'*. There is no indication as to the whereabouts of the one hundred acres, but many of the fields between the West Dean to West Tytherley road and Frenchmoor road had names on the 1836 tithe map which indicated that they were former common land, such as Upper Common, North Common and South Common. They are also in an area of clay soil which would have benefited from being dressed with chalk. Farmers in the 17th and 18th centuries had come to appreciate the value of dressing the fields with a variety of substances to improve the fertility of the soil, and this was facilitated by enclosure. The sheep fold has already been discussed, and another substance which was known to help clay soils particularly was an occasional dressing with chalk to reduce their acidity. Ellis in the 18th century called chalk *'a mineral that is of most exquisite service in farming'* because *'it cures the clays of their sour, cold hard qualities'*, and recommends 25 to 30 loads per acre, each load containing 20 wheelbarrows full. He also recommends that when digging pits to extract the chalk from under the surface soil, they are dug at the edge of fields, in the hedgerow or in woodland, to prevent farm animals getting stuck in the pit, although he admits that most farmers find it more convenient to dig a hole in the middle of the field[24]. Chalk could also be turned into lime, making an even better field dressing and the West Dean tithe map shows one field called Limekiln Field. The 18th century was a time of experiment in improving the yield of crops, and Ellis recommends a range of possible fertilizers which had been shown to give beneficial effects, including dogs' dung, rabbits' dung, the hair of cattle or pigs, woollen rags and horn shavings. There is no record of any such fertilizers being tried locally, but the Dun Valley was fortunate in having good supplies of chalk in fairly close proximity to the areas of clay land which needed it. In addition to the larger chalk quarries there are the remains of many smaller pits, in the middle of fields as well as in the hedgerows and the woodland.

Livestock production

THE IMPROVED HOLSTEIN, OR DUTCH BREED.

SOW OF THE IMPROVED BREED.

Fig. 25 *Improvements in farm animal breeding.* (T. Bewick).

One of the great agricultural advances, which began in the 18th and continued in the 19th century, was the selective breeding of farm animals, and the goal was an animal which produced more meat in a shorter time. In the past cattle had pulled the plough as their primary function and the sheep were kept in large numbers for their wool. The farmers bred their own replacement animals, using the poorer, weaker animals which were less valuable for use on the farm or for sale, as breeding stock. It was only in the 18th century that it was realised that by breeding selectively from the best animals it was possible to change both their conformation, so that they had more muscle meat and less fat on the carcase, and the rate at which they reached maturity. These characteristics could then be improved further by in-breeding. By the 19th century the population of England was rising and becoming more urban, and agriculture needed to change its emphasis and increase its output in order to feed it. Both cattle and sheep were increasingly kept to provide meat, and as transport improved so that milk could reach the towns within a short time, cows became important as producers of liquid milk as well as cheese.

While we have no records of the animals on the Dun Valley farms at that time, there is evidence of the agricultural changes which were needed to support the increased production. Some of the innovations, such as the early spring grass production in water meadows and the addition of chalk and manure to the soil, have been discussed above, while another was the introduction of large-scale turnip growing. Turnips provided food for the animals during the winter months, so that far more cattle and sheep could be kept over the winter, and the old practice of slaughtering large numbers in the autumn was no longer necessary. A survey of the farms on the East Tytherley and Lockerley manor estate in 1829 showed that a number of the farms were growing turnips by that date[25].

The 1829 survey of the farm fields on the manors of East Tytherley and Lockerley not only lists the crops currently under cultivation but also comments on the state of the land, particularly where the drainage was inadequate. During the 19th century much greater efforts were made to drain fields to improve the quality of the grass and the yield of arable crops, either with ditches, or increasingly with drainage tiles under the surface. Some of the worst fields surveyed included;

Eastern Dog Kennel   *Cow pasture, wants trenching, ditches deepened and rushes cut*
North Croft   *Very foul*
Blackmore Mead   *Wants draining badly*
Little Mead   *Sedges and rushes*
Aldermoor   *Alder and timber*

Where the land was particularly difficult to cultivate, especially on areas of heavy clay soil and where the natural drainage was poor, it was often easier to leave it as woodland. However, this was not unproductive land since both timber and coppiced underwood were valuable crops.

Forestry and wood production

The Dun Valley parishes contain many stretches of woodland, not only the 1700 acres of Bentley Wood, most of which lie in West Dean parish, but also smaller woods scattered around the countryside. In 1829 there were 433 acres of woodland on the East Tytherley and Lockerley estate.

In the country as a whole, coppice, with or without standard timber trees amongst it, was still the commonest woodland crop at the beginning of the 19th century, although an increasing number of plantations were being established. The cutting interval of the coppice stools varied, it was most commonly cut after 10-15 years growth, but where hurdles were important in sheep rearing areas it was harvested more often. This was the form of woodland management which would have been so familiar in the Dun Valley woods since man first settled there. Coppiced woodland was cut at regular intervals, and when an area was ready for cutting it was sold in lots as standing coppice. Local woodsmen, and wood craftsmen such as hurdlemakers, would buy a lot containing a few lugs (a variable measure, usually 16 ½ ft. but in woodland often 18ft.) of coppice, which they would cut during the winter months, often with help from their families. Different diameter stems were then used or sold for a variety of purposes. Hurdle makers needed long straight hazel poles of about seven years' growth, thatchers needed hazel spars for holding down the straw on roofs, and bundles of small poles were taken to be used as fuel for bread ovens. A certain number of lugs of the woodland were sold to each woodsman, many of whom had come from villages some distance away.

Plantation woodland was a totally different concept of forestry management which started in the 17th century. Whereas previously both coppiced underwood and the timber trees were grown by natural regeneration in the woodland, followed by active management of the growing trees to select the tree-species and numbers required, plantations were produced by planting seed such as acorns, or young nursery-grown trees, onto an area of cleared ground. This was used as a quicker means of growing timber trees of the desired species precisely where they were required, either as solid blocks of a particular tree species or as alternate rows of different species, so that the more rapidly-growing trees could be cut first, leaving space for slower-growing trees to grow and expand. Coniferous trees such as pine, spruce and fir were introduced, whereas previously softwood timber had been imported, particularly from the Baltic countries. Today we accept such trees as a normal feature of the countryside, but conifer plantations must have looked very alien when they first appeared. The conifers were often alternated with rows of oak trees or other hardwoods, which were slower in reaching the required size, but for which there was always a steady requirement. When the final crop had been taken the land was completely cleared and the whole process repeated. By the 19th century plantations were seen as the way forward for forestry, although there was still a need for hazel coppice.

A survey of woodland on the East Tytherley and Lockerley manor estate in 1829 records the following, which was very different from the woodland as it had been in previous centuries[26]:

East Tytherley and Lockerley - in hand

East Tytherley 443 acres woodland
Plantation - 5 acres, firs
Queenwood & plantation - 13 acres, mostly oak and beech
Timber yard
Great Pullens Plantation - 7 acres, firs with some oak
East Front Plantation - 5 acres, mostly fir, Scotch and larch, no underwood
Lower Horse Leaze Plantation - good plant of small ash
Green House Coppice - 4 acres, all tall oak
The Grove - 5 acres, high timber
South Front Plantation - 2 acres, young timber, good plant of oaks
New Plantation - 2 acres, young firs
Dog kennel Row - 2 acres, young timber
Brick Kiln Wood - 14 acres, ripe high firs, would be fine plant of oak and ash, underwood thinned
Old Fish Pond Bottom - 4 acres, some high firs
Thorns Wood - 15 acres, flitterns thinned, some ash also cut
South Front Plantation - 2 acres, all firs, mostly larch
Part of Thorns Wood - 4 acres, underwood cut, flitterns thinned
Arms? Leaze Plantation - 3 acres, all young oaks, kindly growing
Blackmore Plantation - 16 acres, oak should be planted amongst firs, mostly spruce, no underwood upper part
Thorns Wood - 14 acres, timber
Thorns Wood - 34 acres, timber
Holberry Coppice - 63 acres, timber

Inevitably, plantation forestry was not all plain sailing, or a guaranteed way to make a fortune. The industrial expansion taking place during the 19th century did not depend on the countryside producing wood since the use of coal increased steadily, first as a source of heat, and then as steam power became of greater importance, as a source of mechanical energy. The wooden naval sailing vessels which had been so successful for so long were replaced by iron ships in the late 19th century, and there was no longer a steady demand for timber in the naval dockyards along the south coast. However, there was still a requirement for timber in building construction, and for the produce of the hazel coppices, and woodland continued to play an important part in the economy of the countryside.

10
The Shaping of the Post-Medieval Community

Throughout the Middle Ages life in rural communities had revolved around, and was regulated by, the manor and the church, but from the 16th century onwards there was a gradual change to State administration and control. These were major changes and while they occurred over a few generations, the medieval way of regulating community life eventually changed into something which we would recognise today. Under the Tudor and Stuart kings local government became organised on a county basis, with the hundreds acting as sub-divisions, while the old ecclesiastical parishes had their role changed and expanded to become the smallest administrative units. Central government was firmly in overall control, with all the major county officers being appointed and dismissed by the monarch, and the King's Bench was able to overrule the Justices of the Peace when necessary. All civil officers were required to present themselves at the Assizes before the King's judges and give an account of the maintenance of law and order within the county.

The appointed officers were mainly unpaid, the only paid posts were very minor ones within the parishes, and at different levels involved a significant proportion of the adult men throughout the country. There were just a few officials such as the county Coroner and the Clerk of the Peace who received fees for their work. The services which were demanded by central government and carried out by county officials included organising military service, particularly the Militia for national defence, collecting the taxes which were levied whenever there was a need for more money, maintenance of the peace and the upkeep of main bridges and gaols.

The principal county officer was the Lord Lieutenant, an office which dated from the mid-16th century. Its holder was normally one of the greatest noblemen and it was an appointment for life. Under the Lord Lieutenant were appointments such as deputy lieutenants and the High Sheriff. The county officials which became of particular importance to the inhabitants of rural communities were the Justices of the Peace. The role of these officers was developed and expanded under the Tudors and Stuarts, and they gradually took over many of the judicial and administrative functions within the county. They were nominated by the Lord Lieutenant from among the local noblemen and gentry, and were appointed by the monarch.

To qualify as a potential Justice of the Peace it was necessary to be a £20 freeholder resident in the county, be of the Anglican faith and preferably have some knowledge of law and administration. A General Session of the Peace for the county was held four times a year, which was attended by the Justices of the Peace. Individuals were tried at these Quarter Sessions for breaches of the law, and for many offences which in previous times would have been handled by the manor courts. The Quarter Session was also used as an occasion for the licensing of traders, the regulation of prices and for hearing presentments against parishes or individuals for failure to carry out their duties. The Justices of the Peace were empowered to act individually to summon a person to appear at the Quarter Sessions, and to commit suspects to the county gaol to await trial. They could also punish by fine or the stocks those who were guilty of drunkenness, non-attendance at church or vagrancy.

By the 17th century the parish had become a unit of local government within the larger area of the hundred, in addition to being an ecclesiastical division in which a priest administered to the inhabitants. Service as a parish officer was compulsory and unpaid, and a post was held for one year, or until a replacement was appointed. In some parishes all the men served in rotation, whereas in others only certain landholders served as officers. Peers, clergy, members of the Royal College of Physicians and a few other categories of people were exempt from the duties, which could be both arduous and time-consuming. The parish officers which became part of village life by the 17th century included:

Churchwardens   Between two and four officers who were responsible for the maintenance of the church fabric and churchyard; producing an annual report to the Bishop on the incumbent; the church fabric and the moral state of the church; assisting the other parish officers; levying a church rate on the parishioners for poor-law purposes and keeping good accounts.

Constable   The officer responsible for dealing with vagrants; supervising alehouses; apprehending felons; putting minor trouble-makers in the stocks; making presentments at the Petty and Quarter Sessions and collecting the county rate in the parish.

Surveyor of the Highways   The officer who was responsible for organising compulsory labour from the local population when necessary for road maintenance; for arranging removal of obstructions from the highways and for collecting a highway rate if authorised at the Quarter Sessions.

<u>Overseers of the Poor</u>   A post established in 1597 to be held by 2 – 4 persons whose duties included the relief of destitute people; the removal of paupers without rights of settlement to their former parish; arranging for the care of illegitimate children; organising apprenticeships for destitute children and collecting the poor rate from inhabitants of the parish.

There were also minor paid posts including those of the sexton, hogwarden, pinder (in charge of the village pound), bellringer and parish clerk.

The parish Vestry Meeting was held in the church at Easter, and other times as necessary, and it gradually took over many of the functions of the manor courts. At the meetings the parish officers made by-laws for the parish; administered the village pound and the common pasture; set the church rate to cover repairs to the fabric of the church, and the churchwardens' expenses[1].

The Population of the Dun Valley

Estimating with any degree of accuracy the number of people who lived in an area before the 19th century is difficult. The Domesday survey and lists of householders compiled whenever a tax was imposed are useful indicators, but they include only the heads of households, and do not count all sections of society[2]. Nevertheless, they do provide some idea of how the Dun Valley was populated in the past.

The Domesday survey was based on the populations of manor estates as they existed in 1086, and cannot always be directly compared with later information which was based on parishes. However, the Survey does indicate that West Dean was an entity, a single manor with its tenants living close by and probably forming a small village below the manor house and church. The population in 1086 was listed as[3]: 1 villager (villein), 10 cottagers and 1 serf (slave), to which has to be added their dependent families. East Tytherley manor, which was later held by the Columbars, was held in 1086 by Alwi, son of Saulf. There were 2 villagers, and 9 cottagers[4], and it had therefore a village population similar to that of West Dean. Other areas are more difficult, since the parishes and villages in the Dun Valley, as identified in later centuries, were scattered estates in 1086, and were often held by distant manors.

The number of people in England as a whole rose steadily between 1086 and the late 13th century, even if the population figures are not very exact.

In all areas the number of people was outstripping resources by 1300, and extra land, often on poor quality soil which had previously not been considered to be worth cultivating, now had to become arable fields. There was then a steep drop in the population as a consequence of a series of bad harvests at a time when it was a struggle to feed the high numbers of people, followed by the Black Death. From the 15th century onwards the population rose slowly and steadily.

Taxes levied during the 16th and 17th centuries provide population figures for parishes, which give some idea of the size of the local population and allow a comparison between the parishes. Lay taxes, meaning taxes imposed on the 'lay' as opposed to the ecclesiastical population, on land and goods were imposed at various times during the 16th century. A person who had income from land, including leasehold and copyhold properties and rents, was taxed on the land. Alternatively, people without such assets were taxed on their movable goods, provided that they were worth £3 or more. These taxes were collected on a county basis[5] and the following examples give some idea of the relative population size of the Dun Valley parishes in the 1570s, allowing that only the heads of households are included. The figures also give no indication of the number of people in the poorest section of each parish who did not pay the tax.

Tax payers in the 16th century

1576[6] Deane with Grimsteade   11 names

1571[7] East Tytherley	13 names
Lockerley	12 names
East Dean	11 names
Mottisfont	11 names

Similarly, the Hampshire assessments for the Hearth Tax imposed in 1665 give an indication of the population of the Hampshire parishes a hundred years later (see Appendix II). The Hearth Tax was imposed on the number of chimneys people had, as an indication of their wealth, and is more helpful in that it lists the people who were not charged, in addition to those who were. A rough estimate of the parish population size is 4.5 times the number of householders and it gives some idea of the relative numbers in different sections of society. A person was exempt if he did not pay poor or church rate, his house was worth less than 20s a year, or his land, goods and chattels were worth less than £10 per year. Hearth Tax was charged on the occupier, not the landlord, and less than 3 hearths indicates a fairly low standard of living, while more than 10 indicates considerable affluence. It can be seen from the lists in Appendix II that most families lived in poverty[8].

Approx population in 1665 based on the Hearth Tax

Lockerley	292
East Dean	153
East Tytherley	171

From 1538 onwards the churchwardens were required to keep a record of baptisms, marriages and burials at the parish church. Such records are of interest when tracing the genealogy of specific families, but do not give much information about the total population of an area unless there were very dramatic changes.

Lockerley and East Dean had a combined parish register for most of the 17th century as they were chapels attached to Mottisfont parish. The number of baptisms in the two parishes between 1600 and 1680 varied from 0 to 20 per year, and showed no particular pattern of long-term population change. The numbers of deaths each year also ranged between 0 and 20. There were occasional increases in the deaths in an individual year; for example there were 14 in 1632, 16 in 1644 and 20 in 1680, and there were also periods when for a few years the number of deaths was higher than usual. In most cases the increase was matched by an increase in baptisms, so there may have been many early childhood deaths. The exceptions were 1657, 1658 and 1659 when there were more deaths than usual (17, 11 and 10), but only an average number of births (7, 4, and 7), which might indicate a minor disease outbreak, though there are no indications of a steep rise in deaths due to a major outbreak of plague in the area. The number of marriages was fairly constant at less than 6 per year, except in 1640, when there were 11, and this was accompanied by a rise in births to 13 for that year[9].

There are no entries at all in these registers for the years 1649 and 1650, which may be due to the political chaos around the time when Charles II was brought to trial and condemned to death. The register of East Tytherley shows a similar gap between 1647 and 1651, which may also be due to the Civil War.

The West Dean parish registers had a volume which has been lost, so that there is no comparable information for West Dean and East Grimstead for the whole of the 17th century. G. S. Master, who examined the registers in detail, found some of the missing information in the Salisbury diocesan register, but it was patchy and incomplete. However, parish registers often include a few miscellaneous facts, and Master noted that in 1783 the West Dean register gave the population and the numbers of houses and families in West Dean and East Grimstead as follows[10]:

	West Dean	East Grimstead
Population	185	118
Houses	37	35
Families	35	21

Unfortunately there is no indication as to what constitutes a family; some grandparents could be included with the family, or a widow living alone because the children had moved away, could count as a family. Such information is of interest but cannot be compared with later, more accurate, figures from the 19th century, which were collected in a different way.

Later parish registers give the father's occupation when recording a baptism, and the following list compiled from the East Tytherley parish registers for the period 1813-95 gives an idea of the wide variety of trades within the parish:

Higler (pedlar), Woodman, Carter, Gamekeeper, Blacksmith, Groom, Wheelwright, Steward to F. G. Dalgety esq, Shepherd, Gardener, Sawyer, Licensed Victualler, Policeman, Brickmaker, Warehouseman, Bailiff, Shoemaker, Hospital Porter (1890), Esquire, Butcher, Coachman, Footman, Sweep, Bricklayer, Teacher of English (Queenwood School 1875), Schoolmaster, Publican, Farmer, Dairyman, Engine Driver (1878), Mechanic, Yeoman, and the vast majority – 'Labourer'.

By the 19th century more accurate figures are available since the census returns collected at ten year intervals included the whole population. The first census was collected in 1801 and the early censuses up 1831 were based on the parish overseer's count of the people in the parish; no account was taken of such groups as soldiers, gipsies or people in barges. Later alterations in the boundaries and status of parishes had important effects on the figures, such as when ancient parishes were subdivided into chapelries, hamlets or townships with their own boundaries. The figures for the Dun Valley parishes are shown below, and the population of the surrounding parishes of Broughton, West Tytherley and Mottisfont are given for comparison. There were changes which affected the figures, particularly involving West Dean which had the problem of being spread across the county boundary, and East Grimstead. West Dean was counted as the whole parish before 1851, after which the parts which were in Wiltshire and Hampshire were counted separately. East Grimstead only has a separate count in 1801 when the population was 148, after which it became a chapelry of West Dean.

Parish	1801	1831	1851
East Dean	146	173	207
West Dean	221	360	333
Lockerley	356	560	627
East Tytherley	209	294	399
West Tytherley	488	489	447
Mottisfont	368	515	556
Broughton with Frenchmoor	637	897	1010

Table 1. *Population in the Dun Valley parishes based on census returns*[11]

Table 2. *Population details of the Dun Valley parishes from the 1831 census of England and Wales (the combined area of West Dean and East Grimstead was 2780 acres*[12].

Parish and parish area	Population	Number of houses (uninhabited)	Number of families	Number in agriculture	Number in trade manufacture or handicrafts
East Dean (640 acres)	173	28 (2)	32	21	6
Lockerley (1390 acres)	560	84 (1)	119	98	18
East Tytherley (1560 acres)	294	65 (3)	69	47	13
West Dean	238	58 (0)	59	52	6
East Grimstead	122	27 (0)	28	24	3

Law and Order

During the Middle Ages law and order in rural communities had been maintained by the manor court, except for ecclesiastical matters which were dealt with by the Church courts. Most people, except for freeholders, had been tied to their manor and could not move away to live elsewhere without their lord's permission. They were also bound by the judgments of his court and had no right of appeal in the king's court if they disagreed with the verdict of the manor court.

From the 16th century onwards, following the development of the local government structure described above, law and order became increasingly a matter for the State. By the 17th century most people who had committed offences which had previously been dealt with by the manor court were sent to appear before the Justices of the Peace at the Quarter Sessions.

There was inevitably considerable overlap as the system gradually changed. Brewing ale and breaking the assize by selling ale below the standard strength appears commonly as an offence in the court rolls of the East Tytherley and Lockerley manors in the 16th century, whereas it is not mentioned in the 17th century records, and was presumably being dealt with by the Justices of the Peace by that time. However, in 1655 three tenants of East Tytherley manor appeared before the manor court charged with selling beer without a licence and of disorderly conduct on the Sabbath. The East Tytherley manor court rolls do show the gradual change towards dealing solely with internal estate affairs, but even in the 1670s such offences as flooding the road by obstructing the drainage, and building illegal cottages on the common land were still matters for the manor court (see chap. 6). The Quarter Sessions finally came to deal with the wide range of offences which affected both urban and rural communities, as can be seen from the following list of examples from the Quarter sessions at Winchester[13]:

Running away and leaving his wife and children
Being an idle and disorderly person
Charged as an incorrigible rogue and vagabond
Charged for bastardy
Charged with feloniously taking and carrying away one pair of silver tea-tongs
Profane swearing and lewd behaviour
For assaulting, beating and threatening to rip him up and cut his throat
For stealing a pig out of the yard

For wandering and begging
Having lately been delivered of a female bastard child

These offences were of course from a wide area, and as the population of the Dun Valley in Hampshire was quite low there are correspondingly few entries from the local parishes. However, there were some offences from Lockerley which reached the Winchester Quarter Sessions[14]:

1750   John Rugg
Committed Nov. 20th by Rev. T.Y. Caverley, clerk, charged on the oaths of Thomas Longland and Francis Caines with having privately and feloniously taken and carried away thirteen fowls from out of ye outhouses of the said Thomas Longland and Francis Caines of Lockerley in this county.

1790   Richard Palmer aged 17
Charged on oath with having feloniously stolen, taken and carried away a quantity of cider out of a cellar belonging to a dwelling-house of the Rev. Edward Fleet, clerk, situate in the parish of Lockerley.

1798   Joseph Baker aged 32
Committed Feb 22nd by the Rev. John Penton, clerk, charged on oath with having feloniously stolen and taken away from an out-house, a scythe, the property of Daniel Gass, in the parish of Lockerley. And the said Joseph Baker further stands charged on oath with having feloniously stolen an iron-bound tub, the property of Joseph Rose of Lockerley.

These 18th century Quarter Sessions reports list those charged and awaiting trial in Winchester Castle and do not give the sentences which they eventually received if found guilty, but the sentences were unlikely to have been less severe than they were in the early 19th century, when offences which today would be considered fairly trivial attracted the death sentence. The following are a few examples of the numbers found guilty of capital offences recorded at the 1827 Winchester Lent Assizes[15]:

5 for horse stealing   (age range 19- 29)
6 for sheep stealing   (age range 19- 46)
7 for burglary   (age range 16- 69)
5 for housebreaking   (age range 19- 22)

The deaths were recorded so none had been reprieved.

Provision for those who were destitute was closely connected with the maintenance of public order. Parishes became responsible for the care of the poor and needy within their boundaries, which inevitably meant that they did not want people moving in who had no visible means of support, or who were likely to become a burden on the parish. Legislation was introduced making it illegal for those who could not work to move around at will, and for people to beg outside their own parish. Whereas in medieval times the poorest section of society had been tied to their local manor because it needed their labour, the provision of care for the poor by the parish meant that they were still legally tied to their native village, albeit for different reasons. The concept of State relief for the poor, while at the same time discouraging beggars and vagrants, started under Henry VII, and the latter were punished severely by the Justices of the Peace. In 1495 all *'vagabonds, idle or suspect persons living suspiciously'* were to be put in the stocks for three days and given only bread and water. All beggars not able to work were to go and remain in the hundred where they had last dwelt and stay there, or not to beg[16]. This did not remove the problem, so further legislation was introduced under Henry VIII to ensure that able-bodied beggars and vagrants were severely discouraged. An act introduced in 1531 made it clear that any able-bodied person being vagrant and having no visible means of support was to appear before the Justices of the Peace. If found guilty, he would then be stripped naked from the waist upwards, tied to the back of a cart and beaten with whips around the town until he was bleeding. He was afterwards to return to the place where he had last lived[17].

Fig. 26 *Beating a vagrant tied to a cart. (Punch, 1841)*

During the 17th century many acts were passed attempting to deal with the problems of vagrancy. In 1662 it became illegal for a stranger to move into a parish and settle there unless he rented a tenement of £10, or had evidence of sufficient security not to become a charge on his adopted parish. Otherwise the justices could have him removed forthwith. A temporary residence for work, such as during the harvest, was allowed if the person had a certificate from his own parish, agreeing to take him back. Further legislation followed, and from 1697 poor persons were allowed to enter any parish provided that they produced a certificate from their parish of settlement[18].

The following is from a book of settlement certificates of churchwardens and overseers of the poor[19]:

We John Colence and Thomas Longland, Churchwarden and Overseer of the poor of the parish of Lockerley in the county aforesaid do own and acknowledge Michael Ireland and Ann his wife and also the child or children that the said Ann is now pregnant with, to be inhabitants legally settled in our said parish of Lockerley. In witness whereof we have hereunto put our hands and seals this first day of April in the nineteenth year of the reign of our Sovereign Lord George the Second of Gt. Britain and Ireland, 1746.

Signed   John Collins, Thomas Longland

Others were less fortunate:

Removal Order for Martha Edwards and her children, 1751[20]

Whereas complaint hath been made unto us, two of his Majesty's Justices of the Peace for the county of Southton aforesaid by the Church-Wardens and Overseers of the Poor of the said parish of Lockerley that Martha Edwards, Widow, and Relict of Richard Edwards, deceased, and his five infant children to wit Jane aged about seven years and an half, William aged about five years and an half, Anne aged about three years and an half, Benjamin aged about two years and an half and Martha aged about five weeks lately intruded, and came into the said parish of Lockerley and are like to become chargeable to the same; We the said Justices, upon Examination of the Premises upon Oath and other Circumstances, do adjudge the same to be true, and do also adjudge the Place of legal settlement of the said Martha Edwards, the Widow, and the said Children to be the said parish of Shirefield English.

Relief for the Poor

Although the Tudor monarchs attempted to discourage severely people who were physically able to work from living on charity, they also instituted organised state aid for the elderly, poor and disabled who were unable to provide for themselves. Until that time poor relief had been purely voluntary, with the monasteries in particular playing an important role; this charitable aid naturally disappeared with the dissolution of the monasteries. The Church and local communities also provided voluntary help on a personal basis. The organisation of local government in the 16th century provided for

THE AGRICULTURAL QUESTION SETTLED.

PRIME MINISTER.—" I 'm very sorry, my good man, but I can do nothing for you."

Fig. 27 *The ongoing problem of rural poverty.(J.Leech, in Punch,1845)*

Fig. XIX *The remains of the water channel to the water meadows in East Dean.(AB)*

poor relief within the parishes, under the responsibility of the churchwarden, and administered by designated local officers who had the power to collect money from the rest of the community to pay for it.

At the time when legislation was being put in place to ensure that vagabonds and beggars were whipped and sent back to their home parish, the Tudors also used the same acts of parliament to provide for the genuinely poor and sick. In 1536 it was decreed that churchwardens would collect voluntary contributions on Sundays and feast days and distribute them to the poor and feeble. Destitute children between five and fourteen years of age would be apprenticed, and some of the money collected would be used to buy them a set of clothes to wear when they started[21]. In 1552 parish officers were to be nominated who would collect money to support the poor, and the system of organised relief for those who needed help gradually developed and evolved.

It was not only those at the bottom end of society who needed help. When there was no insurance or old age pension, even a moderately well-off yeoman farmer could fall on hard times as this plea on behalf of Richard Bonner of East Tytherley in 1630 clearly illustrates[22]. He lived for a few more years afterwards, albeit in more restricted circumstances, and his probate inventory (chap. 6) shows that he had a modest collection of belongings at his death in 1638.

To the right hon. Sir Richard Paulet, knight, and the rest of the Justices of her majestie's peace in the county of South(ampton)

In most humble wise sheweth unto your worshipps your pore orator Richard Bonner of the parish of Eastytherlie in the countie of Southt, that whereas upon the 17th day of November laste your sayd orator had his dwelling houses, barnes, stable, all his household stufe, bedding, apparell, all his wheate, barlie, oates and other grayne, his hay and horses to the valew of two hundred markes at the leaste, burned and consumed by misfortune of fyre to his great loste and utter undoing, without the charitable benevolence of well disposed people. These are therefore humbly to beseech your worships in consideration of your said orator's great povertie and impotencie (being olde and darke (blind) and not able in any way to helpe himself in this his greate myserie) to shewe your compation and pitie upon him in granitinge unto your pore orator what favour your wor(ships) may for collecting the charitable devotions of h.. whome god shall move with compation towards the building and reedifyinge his sayd house which otherwise by noe meanes may or can be brought to passe your sayd orator referring himself to your worsh(ips) good and godlie considerations shall continually pray unto thallmyghtie for the elervation of you and everie of you in continuall and everlasting happinesse.

We p(ar)ishoners whose names are here under written certifie your worshipps of the truth

Thomas Ridley   Markes Bettridge   Thomas More   John Pragnell   William Betridge   John Woodford   Robert Goter   George Ireland   George Webb Richard Yeoman   John Barlinge   John Thomas

The Overseers of the Poor for a parish became responsible for providing whatever was required by the very poor, collecting the parish rate from those who could afford it while at the same time trying to prevent anyone settling in the area who might be a financial burden on the parish. The system continued throughout the 18th century, and the range of problems dealt with by the overseers can be seen from their accounts. The following extract from the accounts of the Lockerley Overseer shows the routine outgoings in 1777[23].

Overseers Accounts for Lockerley
Nov. 1777 Disbursments
Pd. Mrs Sleat for Samul Foxes bastard child from the 3 day of August to the 26 Oct which is Twilve week £1 12s
Pd for 3 ...muton for the poor children at 3d per pound 11d
1 gallon best Flower (flour) 11d
Pd Mr Rogers for old Hutchens rent a year and a half up to Micklmas last past 18s 9d
Pd for 2 pare hoas (hose) for the poor children 3s
Pd 2lb Beacen (bacon) for the poor children 1s 3d
Pd Ann Osborn 12 weeks pay due the 23rd day of November 18s
1 gallon best flower 11d
A pare of shoos for Will Spragg 3s 2d
5 pound moten (mutton) for poor children 1s 3d
Paid Thomas Sulence bill for the poor children £14s 7d
Pd for 6 yards of Linsey to meak the poor children pety coats 6s 2d
2 ¼s moten and a pound beacen 1s 2d
1 gallon a flower 11d

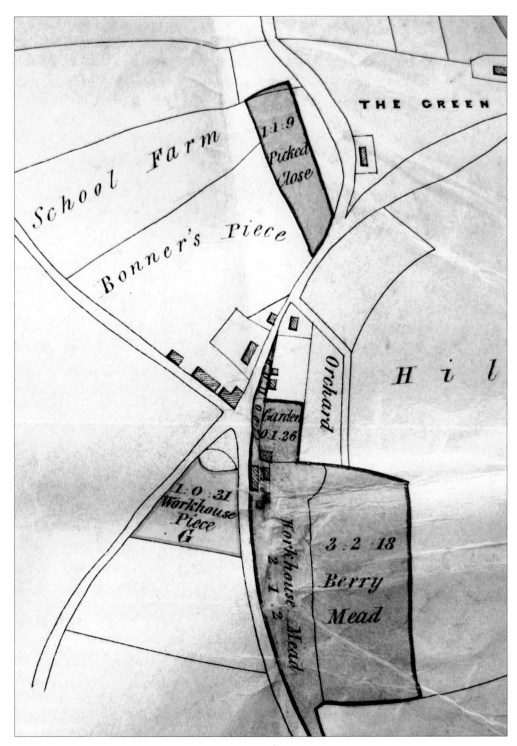

Fig. XX *Map showing the former site of Lockerley Workhouse, 1850. HRO ref.*
5M58/284 Title deeds of land purchased by F. G. Dalgety (AB)

December

Pd for 6 pound Moten at 3 per pound for the poor children	*1s 6d*
Pd for 7 lb muten 3d per pound	*1s 11d*
1 gallon of flower	*11d*
Thomas Sulence bill for the poor children	*£1 4s 10d*
Pd for 3 pound moten for poor children	*9d*
1 gallon best flower for poor children	*11d*

January   1778

Pd for a cheeas for poor children	*11 ½ d*
Pd wido Lawes to by hur shift	*3s*
2 pare stockins for Will Spragg	*1s 1d*
Pd for ... of Moten for poor children	*1s 1 ½ d*
1 gallon flower for the poor children	*11d*
5 pound Cheeas 2 ½ d per pound	*1s ½ d*
Pd Wido Finch when sick	*2s*
Pd for 4 pound Muten for the poor children	*1s*
Pd for 8 ... Cheeas for the poor children	*1s 8 ½ d*
Pd for 2 pound Beacen for the poor children	*1s 3d*
1 gallon Flower	*11d*
Pd old Hutchens	*2s 6d*
Pd Thomas Sulence bill	*£1 5s 6d*
Pd for 2 ½ lbs Becen for the poor children	*1s 8 ½ d*
Pd for ... pound of chees	*2s 11d*
Pd for a coat for Will Spragg	*8s*
Pd for 1 gallon a flower for the poor children	*11d*
	£9 3s 9d

Further records show that the poor were put to work as far as possible, and there are several entries for women spinning, men doing farm work and for a boy picking turnips.

In 1722 the Workhouse Act was passed which provided for the setting up of workhouses in each parish and the provision of poor relief in these workhouses only. This change was to make it easier to provide relief, by buying or renting a house for the lodging of the poor of the parish, and to use their work and labour to maintain the house. Sixty years later Gilbert's Act of 1782 permitted parishes to combine together for more effective administration. Work was to be provided for the able-bodied poor, with wages supplemented from the poor rate if necessary. Only the infirm would be sent to the workhouse.

It is not clear what accommodation was set up in the separate Dun Valley parishes during the earlier part of the 18th century, but the above Overseer's account suggests that the children at least were being provided for communally. Whatever was being provided in the separate local parishes was apparently not ideal, because in 1791 it was agreed at a vestry meeting that a joint Poor House would be provided for the poor people of Lockerley, East Dean and Mottisfont[24]. A convenient house would be found in Lockerley for lodging the poor of the three parishes, and another house, or outhouses, would be used for the poor to work in and to store fuel. There was also to be a garden sufficient to supply the house with everything that could be grown there. A Master and Mistress were to be appointed, and to be paid to superintend the house. Pregnant single women seem to have been something of a problem and how they were to be dealt with was set out at some length. They were not to be admitted into the general poor house, but were to be sent 'to lie in their respective parishes'. Any bastard child which was born unexpectedly in the poorhouse in Lockerley would be entitled to the settlement of the mother.

The house was agreed upon, and a little later John Dowling and his wife Sarah were appointed as the Master and Mistress of the house.

It was agreed between the parishioners of the 3 parishes to rent the house of Mr John Atkins, with the stable adjoining and the 2 little gardens now let with the same, at the yearly rent of seven pounds, and if more garden be wanted it is agreed to pay the said Mr Atkins 3 pence annually.

In 1830 the house, 'lately used as a Poor House', was given back to the then owner[25]. The site was still called Workhouse Piece on the tithe map in 1840, and on an 1850 map of that part of Lockerley (Fig.XX, p158).

During the second half of the 18th and the early 19th centuries there were many attempts throughout the country to find ways of relieving poverty in a constructive way among the poorest section of society. These included trying to find, or create, work for the unemployed, and providing money from the parish to supplement low wages. The money given was related to the current price of bread, as the rise and fall in wheat prices had a major impact on the cost of living for the poor. A wide variety of parish workhouses had been built, which were originally intended for unemployed labourers, but which were also used to accommodate children, the aged or sick and the mentally handicapped. There was also a lack of uniform policy, leading to much variation in both outdoor relief and the parish workhouses.

The problems of widespread poverty continued, as they had done for many centuries, and by 1834 general discontent with the existing poor laws resulted in the Poor Law Amendment Act. By this a national system of workhouses was introduced, which was to provide separate accommodation for children, the aged and infirm, able-bodied males and able-bodied females. The hundreds were divided into districts, or unions, and a separate workhouse was provided in each. Existing buildings were often used for one or other of the categories of pauper, so there could be three or four individual workhouses within a single union. By 1841 many new multiple-use workhouses were being constructed, with separate accommodation for the segregation of different classes of inmates. Most workhouses provided temporary space for the assorted itinerant tramps, homeless persons and seasonal labourers which were included under the umbrella term 'vagrants'. It was decreed that from henceforth no outdoor relief would be provided, although this was not universally enforced[26].

In the Dun Valley paupers from West Dean, East Tytherley, West Tytherley and Broughton were to go to the Stockbridge Union workhouse, while East Dean, Lockerley and Mottisfont were in the Romsey Union. East and West Grimstead were part of the Alderbury Union and in 1884 West Dean was transferred to Alderbury. The conditions provided in the union workhouses were to be sufficiently harsh as a policy so that they would deter people from wanting to go there except as a last resort. The Victorian approach to the management of the poor, when viewed from the 21st century, seems hard and cruel, particularly such aspects as the segregation of children away from their parents, but leaving children among adults in a mixed communal workhouse would probably have been even worse. Modern 'enlightened' social care still has not found the ideal way of dealing with the problems of the lower reaches of society, so it is hardly surprising if the Victorian system seems with hindsight to be less than desirable.

Although poor relief became the responsibility of local government, charity continued to play an important part, just as it does today. The lord of the manor and other prominent local inhabitants of the parish often left provision in their wills for money from their estate to be distributed to the poor each year, either as money or as food, clothing or other necessities.

Fig. XXI *The Winchester to Old Sarum Roman road in wet weather. (AB)*

In 1684 Sir John Evelyn of West Dean bequeathed the sum of £20, charged on the Dean estate and to be distributed at the discretion of the lord of the manor as follows;

To the poor of the parish of West Dean £8, East Grimstead £4, Whiteparish £4, Broughton £4

In West Dean it was distributed to anyone in need, except bad characters, and given in proportion to the size of the families. It was generally given in money, but occasionally partly as fuel[27].

An alternative way of leaving provision for the poor in a will was to bequeath property or land. In 1730 Edward Thistlethwaite, gent, left a cottage and 13 acres of land in East Grimstead, the rent from which was to be divided between those in need who were not in receipt of poor relief, at the discretion of the minister, churchwardens and the overseer of the poor[28]. These two charities were still in operation in the 19th century. In addition to major bequests, many people of modest means left small sums in their wills for the local poor and needy.

Education

The ability to read and write was not of major importance in rural communities before the 18th century. The gentry, the doctor, the parson and a few others such as the lord of the manor's steward and certain parish officials were literate, but for everyone else practical skills were valued more highly. The 16th and 17th century probate inventories of gentlemen,

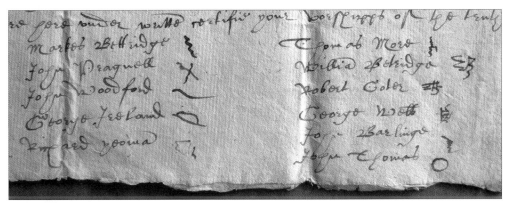

Fig. 28 *Signed by a mark , East Tytherley,1630. HRO, Jervoise of Herriard Collection, 44M69/G3/203 (AB)*

priests and a doctor in the Dun Valley included some books, particularly the bible, but books were not listed among the belongings of anyone else, even quite well-off yeomen farmers. The petition in 1630 on behalf of Richard Bonner (see above) was signed by twelve prominent East Tytherley villagers, and eleven of the twelve could not write their names and signed with a mark (Fig. 28). The marks are interesting in that each one was different and was probably well known within the local community, providing a simple substitute for writing on the few occasions on which it was required. Some people would have been able to read and most of them would have been able to count, add and subtract in their heads or using counters, and may have known the symbols for the numbers, skills which even craftsmen and lowly labourers would have needed for everyday life. Shepherds would have been as speedy at adding up how many sheep were missing as market traders were at counting the day's takings.

Although there was no shame attached to illiteracy, by the early 17th century the more prosperous farmers were farming for profit rather than just subsistence and needed to keep accounts, and transactions such as land conveyance and other legal agreements increasingly used written documents. The ability to read and write therefore gradually became a useful asset even in rural areas. It was also of value when younger sons of farming families wanted to pursue other ways of earning their living than by tilling the soil.

As literacy increased the idea of educating the poorer sections of society developed, although the motives for helping them were perhaps a little different than they would be today. Early education was mainly religious instruction, to give children a familiarity with the scriptures and catechism according to the denomination of their household or community. The aim was to teach the poor to be honest, hardworking, humble and submissive by teaching them to read. Some writing and arithmetic was also taught, but these were considered less important, and instruction was often given in simple skills such as spinning and knitting.

Many charity schools were set up around the country during the 18th century which gave children the opportunity for education which their parents would never have had. Although it was accompanied by the underlying idea that children needed to be taught their station in life, in most cases they must have reaped the benefits. A charity school was founded in 1718 in East Tytherley by Sarah Rolle, daughter of Sir Francis

Rolle who owned the manors of East Tytherley and Lockerley. Her earliest move was in 1717 when she arranged a lease on a piece of land in East Tytherley to build the planned school[29], which was to be situated on the border of Lockerley parish so that it was convenient for children from both directions. The date of the foundation is recorded as 1718[30], but the site of the school was changed and it was actually built much nearer to East Tytherley village, where the old school house still stands today, much altered into a private residence, Rolle House. In 1725 it was recorded in the reply to the bishop's visitation to East Tytherley that a charity school had been founded by Sarah Rolle, spinster, and at that date it had 40 scholars, under the direction of Peter Barber, the master[31].

Sarah Rolle endowed the school and later in 1736 a charitable trust was set up by deed, naming the trustees who were to control the finances[32]. The trust included not only the school site in East Tytherley but also Lockerley Farm, later called School Farm, as a source of revenue. The school was to provide education for children between 6 and 14 years of age, half from East Tytherley and half from Lockerley. They were to be taught to write a good hand and to count, and the boys were to be taught the principles of the Church of England and the church catechism, and to behave soberly. The girls were also to be instructed in the religious principles, and to 'read, worke plaine worke, knit, and marke and flourish muslin'. Clothes were to be provided for each child, and there was a daily allocation of bread and cheese[33].

The only other village in the area with a charity school at an early date was Broughton, where Thomas Dowse had founded a school in 1601. Education for the masses slowly gathered momentum as more schools around the country were founded by private individuals or groups, who by the 19th century were able to obtain liberal state grants to help with the building and maintenance. The National Society for Educating the Poor in the Principles of the Established Church was particularly successful and founded many schools, including the school in East Dean as well as West Tytherley school, which was opened in 1855. However, since education was purely voluntary until after the Elementary Education Act 1876, the provision of schools before that time was very haphazard and some areas were much better served than others

Lockerley school was opened as an extension of the East Tytherley endowed charity school in 1870. It was at this time that legislation was brought

ELEMENTARY EDUCATION ACT, 1870.
Sections IX., XLIX., LI.

Notice C. B.

COUNTY OF **HANTS.**

SCHOOL DISTRICT OF **LOCKERLEY.**

CONTRIBUTORY DISTRICT.

WHEREAS the Education Department, in pursuance of the Elementary Education Act, 1870, have received the Returns in the said Act mentioned, and made such inquiry as they think necessary with respect to the School accommodation of the District hereinafter mentioned; Now, therefore, the Lords of the Committee of Council on Education have decided, and

Hereby give Notice as follows :—

I. The School District is the Parish of **LOCKERLEY.**

II. It is proposed to make the District contribute to the provision and maintenance of a School in the District of **EAST DEAN**, in respect of the number of children named in the second Schedule to this Notice.

III. The School named in the first Schedule to this Notice is considered to be available for the District.

IV. Additional Public School accommodation of the amount and description mentioned in the second Schedule to this Notice appears to be required for the District.

SCHEDULE I.

Name and Description.	Situation.	No. of Children accommodated.			
		Boys.	Girls.	Infants.	TOTAL.
Endowed School - -	Lockerley -	89			89
				TOTAL -	89

SCHEDULE II.

Amount and description of accommodation required.	Situation.	Particulars.
For 23 children (in respect of whom it is proposed to make this parish contributory to East Dean).	East Dean - -	If the East Dean National School be again conducted as a Public Elementary School under a certificated teacher, no further accommodation will be required.

EDUCATION DEPARTMENT,

12th day of February 1873.

Notice No. 4,850.

Union of ROMSEY.

F. R. Sandford

Secretary.

Fig. 29 *Form issued under the Education Act, 1870. HRO ref. 127M83/PJ13 (AB)*

Fig. XXII *Bridge over the old canal, East Grimstead. (AB)*

Fig. XXIII *Site of the old canal wharf, West Dean. (AB)*

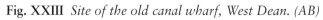

into force dividing counties into school districts, and it was the duty of the county Committee of Education to satisfy themselves that the provision of elementary education in each of these districts was adequate[34], as can be seen in Fig. 29. The school was subsequently enlarged in 1886. The following are a few extracts from the Minutes Book of the school managers 1870-83[35].

Aug. 1871   All articles of school furniture, such as masters desk, bookcase, chairs, books, slates and all other indispensible requisites to be forthwith procured.
Oct. 1871   Ida Southwell to be engaged to teach needlework.
Dec. 1873   It was ordered that children of the higher standard in the school be taught to write in copy books instead of slates as hitherto.
Sept. 1874   Henceforth all children above seven years of age shall write their dictation and other exercises on paper books, to be paid for by such children at ½ d each.

1878   There was a visit by Her Majesty's Inspector of Schools who made 'several observations', showing that bureaucracy had already penetrated the education system. The minutes include the school manager's comments on his report:

In the first place it is compulsory to have hanging up conspicuously in the school a certain extract of the Education Act.
There must be a log book belonging to the school. The inspector found fault at our being without one, as the Government consider it necessary. The inspector also found fault that our Admission Register has no index in it. It will be necessary for the Government Inspector to examine any children whose parents may wish (them) to go to work, to grant a certificate. Unless the regulations are carried out this school will not be recognised as a Public Elementary School and in this case would compel this parish to build a Board school for the 89 children who come here.

March 1882   It was reported that Edward Finch was suspended for disobedience involving a catapult, to the risk of accident to the younger children.
William Bennett and Robert Bennett were expelled for non-payment of the regular school fees and for irregular attendance.

Sept. 1882   In consequence of the Schoolmaster's children having taken scarlet fever during the holidays ... and of two cases of it having been reported in the parish, it was determined with advice of the Sanitary Inspector to close the school until Oct. 2nd.

East Dean also had a school. It originated in 1853, was established as a National school in 1855 and the school minutes record the exact dimensions of the building provided:

	Length	Breadth	Height
Schoolroom	27ft. 6ins.	16ft. 3ins.	18ft.
Classroom	12ft. 2ins.	8ft. 2ins.	14ft. 10ins.

All seemed well at the start, in 1858 Her Majesty's inspector of schools and the inspector of the National Society visited the school and reported that *'East Dean is a good specimen of a village school, that the building is commodious and well situated and sufficiently supplied with apparatus'*.

Twenty years on the school minutes had a rather despondent tone since a report in 1878 had commented that: *'The arithmetic is not satisfactory. The reading is monotonous and difficult to follow, owing to rapidity and disregard of stops. The writing is fair and the general order and discipline not amiss. The children should be taught to speak out distinctly.'* The report continues: *'My Lord hath ordered the grant be reduced by one tenth under Article 32(b) for defective instruction in arithmetic.'* Problems in primary schools are obviously nothing new. However, the 1883 report is rather more encouraging: *'The school is in good order and the character of the attainments continues to be creditable, more intelligence in the reading is desirable in some classes'*[36].

Following the Elementary Education Act and the general move to provide basic education for all children within reasonable distance from their homes, many more villages set up schools, and both West Dean and East Grimstead had their own schools by that time.

The Role of Women

Throughout the Middle Ages and afterwards young single country girls from families below the status of yeomen frequently worked as live-in servants or wage labourers. Such work was often found at the hiring fairs which were common throughout the country and many young girls moved into other areas or to the nearest towns as servants. Further up the social scale unmarried girls remained in their parents' household and took part in the work there. The majority of women then married and became part of a household, which was usually made up of the married couple and a

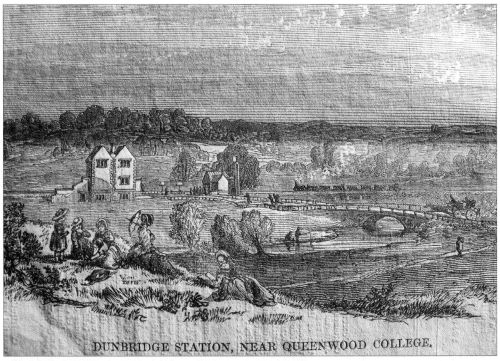

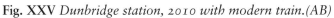

Fig. XXIV *Dunbridge station, 1849, from the Queenwood Reporter. HRO ref. 47M72 (AB)*

Fig. XXV *Dunbridge station, 2010 with modern train.(AB)*

small number of children. Extended family groups including grandparents and other family members were not common and the older children moved out to become apprentices or live-in servants in their early teens. When she married the country woman took on a wide range of domestic tasks as well as responsibilities in the farmyard and field. The essential work included making cheese, baking the bread and brewing the ale. There was also the herb garden to cultivate and the clothes to wash, as well as helping with the outdoor tasks, and whenever there was time to spare the wool was waiting to be spun or some knitting to be finished. The exact range of her occupation naturally depended on her status in society, the yeoman farmer's wife having a larger domestic establishment to organise than the wife of a labourer[37].

Women often brought some money into the household by selling surplus produce in the local market, or by brewing beer. Brewing fitted into the domestic routine and married women were often the village brewsters. They also worked for the lord of the manor and Augustine Stevens's accounts for East Tytherley manor in 1680 (chap. 7) include payments to women for doing the washing, work in the garden and for winnowing the wheat and barley.

Although a woman's wealth became her husband's property when she married, a situation which was only legally abolished in 1882, she was provided for in the event of his death. In Tudor and Stuart times it was customary for a woman to be endowed with either specific property or a third of her husband's holdings on the day of the marriage, to which property she also had full rights for the duration of her lifetime. A familiarity with the outdoor farm work was vital in an age when widowhood was very common, and the woman was often left managing the tenancy. Having paid the heriot (the best beast) to the lord of the manor, the widow received the tenancy through the manor court, to which she then swore fealty. Although women did not normally take part as jury members at the manor court proceedings, widows were expected to do so.

During the 17th century widows often featured in the East Tytherley and Lockerley manor court rolls. The entries are commonly for taking over a tenancy, or for failing to attend a court meeting, but widows were not infrequently found guilty of the usual crimes which occupied court time, such as failure to dig out drainage ditches, inadequate property maintenance and erecting cottages illegally on the common land.

11
Travel and Transport

Roads

Today we take the ability to travel around Britain, and further afield, for granted, but in historical terms this is a very recent development. People did make long journeys even in prehistoric times, but travelling was a major undertaking rather than an everyday event.

The Romans moved their armies over long distances throughout their empire, and built a network of substantial roads to enable them to do so. Such roads were constructed by building a raised bank, or 'agger' with drainage ditches at the sides, and the road ran along the top. As a conquering military force the Romans had ample labour for carrying out the work, and no need to negotiate with the native inhabitants about the route which a road should take. Consequently the Roman road was built in a straight line towards its destination, except where there was a steep hill to negotiate. They also built bridges across the rivers, and causeways to traverse persistently waterlogged ground. The building materials varied, depending on what stone was available locally, and stones were cut to size and arranged in layers to make a firm, well-constructed foundation for the road. Across the downland country and river valleys between Winchester and Salisbury chalk, flint and gravel were readily available for constructing roads[1]. The remains of the Roman road between Winchester and the old site of Salisbury at Old Sarum are still visible. Many stretches of it underlie lanes and tracks which we use today, and in places the remains of the road can be seen as a long bank through the woodland. This major highway ran just to the north of the Dun Valley, and it remained in use as an important route long after the Romans retreated from our shores. In Norman times Winchester was the seat of power in England and the site of Old Sarum was fortified to become a strategically important city. In the 13th century a hunting lodge at Clarendon, a few miles south-east of Salisbury, was developed as a royal palace, and the old Roman road allowed medieval kings and their retinues to reach the palace and its surrounding hunting forests without too much difficulty. The existence of this Roman road meant that Waleran at West Dean, and other Norman noblemen, could reach Winchester by a fairly direct route. The Roman crossing point of the river Test near Horsebridge was abandoned after the Romans left, which diverted travellers to either Kimbridge or to Stockbridge to cross the river. In the Middle Ages many noblemen held widely-scattered estates around England, to which they travelled from time to time, and their servants and messengers would also have journeyed from one to another. However, there was very limited trade and movement of goods, and most estates and villages had an almost self-sufficient economy. There was some need to move commodities which could not be obtained locally, such as salt and iron, and sparsely-forested areas, such as the Wiltshire downland, depended on transporting timber and firewood from distant woodland. Large quantities of wood from Bentley Wood in West Dean parish were hauled to Amesbury manor, which owned part of the wood, and Amesbury priory was also supplied with wood on a regular basis[2].

The mobility of most villagers in rural areas was restricted to travelling to markets and fairs, moving animals to seasonal grazing areas, or driving their pigs to pannage in woodland some distance away for a few weeks in the autumn. Most of the traffic on the roads was very local, moving around within the estate or parish. In addition, the population of the countryside was not very great, which helped to reduce the wear on the road surfaces. Nevertheless, the roads were often in a very poor state, particularly during the winter months. Roads on the well-drained chalk hills were easier to travel along than those in the low-lying marshy valleys, and areas of heavy clay soil also became very hard to traverse during the winter. Consequently long-distance routes often made use of chalk ridgeways, such as Dean Hill. This prominent ridge was part of an ancient well-recognised track leading westwards to the Avon Valley, and beyond. The bishop of Winchester owned Downton and its surrounding estates, so that during the Middle Ages there was movement backwards and forwards using the hilltop route which still exists today as an unsurfaced track[3]. Roads on lower ground were adequate for moving around locally to and from the fields and between villages, and they often formed part of longer routes to markets. During the drier months of the year the valley roads could also be used for longer journeys and travellers who used the route along the top of Dean Hill in winter may well have used the lower roads along the Dun Valley during the summer.

Road transport

Strings of packhorses had always been the principal method of transporting goods over long distances, and were still used in the 18th century. Although carts were used for local journeys, such as taking the hay or sheaves of corn back from the fields to the farmyard, they were of limited use on roads which were sometimes awash with lying water and deep mud, or lethally slippery on steep slopes where the chalk layer was exposed. Nevertheless, carriers, using either packhorses or carts, did operate regular services along the main routes around England throughout the Middle Ages. During the 17th century two-wheeled carts were replaced by more robust four-wheeled wagons, each wagon pulled by several horses. The horses were harnessed together in a line in front of the wagon. This was less efficient than pulling in pairs, but the roads, inn gateways and town streets were often not wide enough to allow two horses abreast, in addition to the waggoner, who walked or rode alongside on a horse to control the team.

Most travellers did not move around in vehicles, many of the poorer people went on foot, while the better-off rode on horseback. Both men and women rode horses, the women often riding pillion. In 1638 the probate inventory of Robert Tutt, gentleman, of Lockerley, included a pillion saddle for his wife to sit on behind him. People sometimes travelled long distances on horseback as well as just locally, and on a long journey they could average about 40 miles per day. Coaches were developed from wagons during the 17th century, and when travelling along the main routes between London and the principal towns and cities, this provided another option for those who could afford it. The journey time was reduced considerably by changing horses at regular staging posts, so that coach horses were worked harder for a short distance, and this became the stage-coach. Originally the coach body was suspended by leather straps from the frame, which were later replaced by steel springs. The coach was a light vehicle, carrying six passengers and usually pulled by four horses in pairs, which could be controlled by a driver riding on the coach. When six horses were needed because of the road conditions, a postilion rode on one of the front horses, as the front two were too far forward to be controlled by the coach driver. The nobility and very wealthy did not, of course, travel in public vehicles, they had their own private coaches[4].

Maps

Old maps, which were usually produced on a county basis, give some idea of routes through the Dun Valley which might have been used in the past, but the roads shown on them are often somewhat inaccurate, and before the 18th century maps frequently did not show roads at all. Rivers were usually shown fairly accurately, as were other features regarded as important, particularly the position of gentlemens' estates and parks. Map makers did not always carry out a detailed survey, and relied on copying details from existing maps, so that mistakes were regularly perpetuated[5].

Ogilby in 1675 mapped the connection between every seaport and London, and produced diagrammatic itineraries for intending travellers. He included a route from London to Weymouth, which was also the way to Dorchester, the county town of Dorset. Rather than showing the well-used road through Andover and Salisbury, his recommended route went via Basingstoke, crossed the Test at Stockbridge, and then went through Broughton, West Tytherley and West Dean, before climbing Dean Hill and continuing along the old tracks to Downton (Fig. 30). From there his route crossed the Avon and headed for Cranborne. West Dean on the county boundary was mistakenly called East Dean in this itinerary. The recommended route had to make a detour across to Whiteparish instead of following the hills directly to Downton, since what is now National Trust land on Pepperbox Hill was at that time private land belonging to Brickworth House. Although the roads which Ogilby recommended existed and were well-used locally, there is no record of it being used as a regular through route from London to Weymouth[6].

The confusion between East and West Dean was perpetuated on the map of the county of Hampshire by Thomas Kitchin in 1751 (Fig. 31), made even more inaccurate by East Dean being shown as well to the south of the river Dun, almost on the Salisbury to Romsey road. The early 19th century one inch-to-the-mile Ordnance Survey Old Series maps, are more

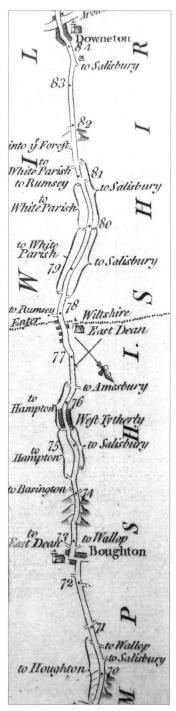

Fig. 30 *Part of Ogilby's itinerary from London to Weymouth,1675. HRO ref. 139M89/2/52 (AB)*

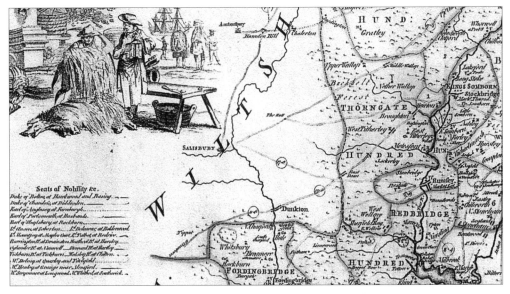

Fig. 31 *Map of Hampshire, 1751. (T. Kitchin)*

useful, although they still have some anomalies. They are not based on individual counties, which is helpful when investigating an area which lies across a county boundary, and the map gives a good idea of the Dun Valley roads in about 1806 when the area was surveyed. However, no maps before the first edition Ordnance Survey maps produced in the 1870s, can be relied upon to show all the roads accurately. These new maps, particularly the large-scale 25 inches to-the-mile maps, were extremely accurate and show a tremendous degree of detail.

Road maintenance

The surface of roads which were used regularly by people on horseback, packhorses or wheeled vehicles, particularly during wet weather, soon became poached or rutted so that water did not drain away. Following heavy rain, where the subsoil was chalk this became exposed on any steep incline, as the water running down the slope cut a narrow stream in the road surface, leaving slippery chalk and loose flints on the surface. The water then lay in a lake on the track at the bottom of the hill. The problems can be seen today on the old tracks which have never been surfaced, and have remained as green lanes or byways (Fig. XXI, p162).

When the monasteries were wealthy thriving enterprises they took responsibility for maintaining many of the roads, particularly those which the monks needed as routes to their outlying estates and granges. Mottisfont was probably no exception, and may have helped to ensure that the roads along the Dun Valley leading to their East Dean estate were kept in a usable state. It is probable that several different tracks were used, and as both Lockerley and East Dean were part of Mottisfont parish, their churches being attached to Mottisfont church, there would have been well-used ways across to both villages. What are now tracks across the fields and woodland would probably have been easier, drier routes than those along the valley beside the river.

Following the dissolution of the monasteries, the condition of roads throughout the country deteriorated, and this was exacerbated by an increased population and a general increase in mobility during Tudor and Stuart times. In 1555 legislation was introduced making parishes responsible for road maintenance. Parishioners had to give four consecutive days labour a year to carry out road repairs under an appointed highways officer, and this was later increased to six days. The officer was to inspect the parish roads, water-courses and bridges three times a year. From the end of the 17th century a parish levy provided for hired labour instead of unpaid service. Road maintenance continued to be a parish responsibility until 1894, when it was transferred to district councils[7].

Following the enclosure of Butlers Wood in 1815, the access roads to farms which had previously crossed the common land had to be established, and arrangements made for their upkeep. In 1815 a schedule was drawn up setting out the proportion of the maintenance costs which were to be paid by the principal holders of the newly-enclosed land. An area of land was allocated to the Lockerley parish surveyor of highways for a chalk or gravel pit for road maintenance[8].

Droves

Droves, or driftways, were tracks used for moving groups of animals around the countryside, the animals being driven together as a herd, rather than restrained as packhorses, draught horses or oxen. Whereas a track used by ridden or packhorses could be quite narrow in places, droves were always very wide. The term 'drove' was used for local tracks which were used for moving the combined village flock or herd to and from their common grazing pastures; it was also used to describe long-distance tracks for driving cattle and sheep to markets and fairs. Such roads were not maintained by any authority, and were not subject to any tolls.

A drove leading to a village from the local common land was characteristically funnel shaped where it left the open ground, as the animals which had been spread out gathered together, poaching the ground as they did so, and ran into the hedged track leading to the village. The name 'drove' often persisted after enclosure of the common land, when the farm animals were retained in the individual farmers' fields and no longer moved as a common herd or flock under the direction of the village shepherd or cowherd. Former droves can therefore often be identified today around the local countryside. The road leading out of West Dean towards West Tytherley has Drove Farm alongside it, and Long Drove leads out of East Grimstead towards Ben Lane. When both these areas are located on the tithe maps, it is noticeable that most of the fields surrounding the droves have names denoting former common land. Further down the Dun Valley, Drove Copse indicates the position of a drove passing through it and leading across from Mottisfont to Lockerley and East Tytherley.

Long-distance drove routes led to fairs and markets, and when there were very large sheep flocks grazing the downlands of Wiltshire and Hampshire, professional drovers moving sheep along the drove tracks to the sites of major fairs, such as Weyhill or Wilton, would have been a familiar sight. Cattle, pigs and even geese were also regularly driven to markets many miles away. Occasional ponds, where animals could drink, were a feature of droves and when there was a river to cross, the drove led to a suitable place for a ford. Long-distance routes had overnight accommodation for the drovers, with paddocks for the animals nearby, such as the Winterslow Hut, later called The Pheasant, on the present A30, which later became a coaching inn. Shorter tracks led from the villages to join the major droving routes[9].

Turnpike or toll roads

As trade and the movement of goods increased during the 17th and 18th centuries, so too did the volume of traffic on the roads, and parishes were increasingly unable to keep their roads in a reasonable state. Where a major road ran across the parish, the villagers were unwilling constantly to repair damage caused by through traffic. In addition to the increased volume of traffic, the size and weight of vehicles using the roads was increasing, and heavy four-wheeled wagons carrying large loads, each pulled by several horses, damaged the road surfaces to a far greater extent than smaller two-wheeled carts. The levying of a toll to pay for the upkeep of a main highway began in 1663, when the first Turnpike Act was passed, and this was followed by further Acts in the 17th century. The idea was successful

Fig. 32 *17th century coach (Thrupp, 1877)*

and the number of turnpike roads increased steadily, each one preceded by an Act of Parliament, which established the particular turnpike trust, and empowered the trustees to erect gates, collect tolls and to borrow money in order to carry out the maintenance work required before a toll could be levied. The number of new Turnpike Acts reached a peak between 1750 and 1770, during which time the main roads which affected the Dun Valley were turnpiked[10].

Salisbury – Basingstoke – Stockbridge - Lopcombe Corner   1755-6
Salisbury – Southampton   (via Eling near Redbridge)   1753
Salisbury – Southampton   (via Whiteparish and Romsey)   1755-6

The turnpike trusts made improvements to pre-existing roads by renovating the road surfaces and digging drainage ditches on each side. Where the road went over a very steep hill a new section of road was sometimes constructed to reduce the gradient. Toll roads were usually about six yards wide, although the surface was not always metalled across the whole width, and they were wide enough for horses to be harnessed abreast when pulling a wagon or coach.

The tolls were collected by a toll collector, who lived in a cottage by the tollgate. A tollhouse was usually built with a polygonal front or projecting central bay to accommodate extra windows, which gave a good view in both directions. Every tollhouse had to display a list of the tolls charged, since different charges were made for different classes of traffic. Vehicles were charged according to how many horses were pulling them, and animals being driven through as a herd were charged according to species and number. Some traffic was exempt from tolls, such as agricultural vehicles, soldiers and churchgoers. Milestones were erected along all toll roads, showing the distance from the last town passed through, and the next one along the road, and the distance from London was often given as well for good measure[11].

During the mid-18th century, when turnpiking was at its height, some roads began to be included which were not part of major routes to London, but were useful cross-country links to the bigger roads. In 1765 the roads from Romsey to Stockbridge and Wallop became toll roads, including roads running through the Dun Valley parishes, as outlined below[12].

From Awbridge to the garden wall of Denys Rolle esq. at East Tuderley; and from Lockerley Mill Stream to East Dean Gate; and from the the said garden wall to the Turnpike Road leading from Stockbridge to Salisbury.

The toll charges were given as follows:

For every horse or other beast, drawing any carriage	4 ½ d
For every horse or other beast, laden or unladen, and not drawing any carriage	1 ½ d
For every ox, cow or neat cattle	¾ d
For every calf, hog, sheep or lamb	½ d

The payment was per day, and allowed the animal to pass toll-free through the same gate and through all other gates on the same roads later in the day. However;

Stage coaches and other carriages taking goods or passengers for pay or reward pay every time of passing.

There are several references to this new turnpike road during the 18th and early 19th centuries. A document dated 1778[13] refers to the track over

Whiteshoot Hill as a turnpike, and confirms that the deep track next to it was the old road. The indenture of the sale of Norman Court to Charles Wall in 1806 mentions 'the new turnpike road over Whiteshoot Hill'[14]. In 1801 an agreement between William Wakeford and Daniel Gass of Lockerley to exchange two pieces of land refers to the road leading northward out of Lockerley to East Tytherley as 'the turnpike road'[15].

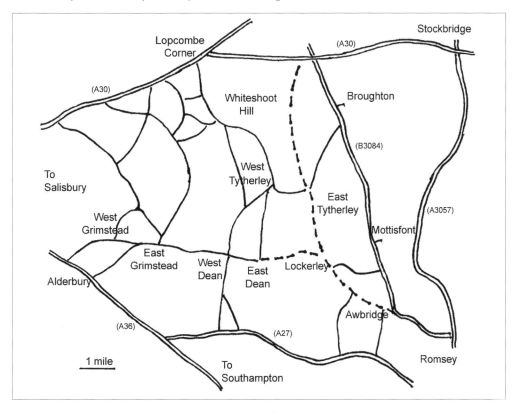

Fig. 33 *Local tollroads.(MB)*
⌐ *Turnpike roads.* --- --- --- *The turnpike road through Lockerley and East Tytherley.*

The maps of that period, which differentiate between turnpikes and side roads, do not show this particular road as a toll road, but they may not have included the less important turnpike routes, and maps were not noted for always being entirely accurate anyway. Further confirmation of the presence of a turnpike road through East Tytherley can be found in the reports of the Swing Riots. In 1830 a mob destroyed the turnpike gates at East Dean and East Tytherley and burnt down the toll houses[16]. The payment of tolls to maintain roads was not universally popular, particularly among the lower classes who regarded them as being a creation of the rich and powerful, and who were already inflamed by what they saw as the iniquities of enclosure of the countryside, which was happening around the same time[17]. A rioting mob on the rampage, as during the Swing Riots, would have seen tollgates as an opportunity to make another important political point.

The development of the railways led to a rapid decline in the formation of new turnpike trusts from about 1870 onwards, and existing trusts became increasingly insolvent as the railways began to take some of the traffic. From 1871 the annual Parliamentary Committees on Turnpike Bills were winding up the trusts as quickly as possible, and transferring the maintenance of the roads to the local authorities. A series of Highways Acts created Highway Districts within each county to oversee the roads, and by the 1880s the maintenance of all the important roads was a county responsibility, and the county surveyor had the authority to inspect all roads classified as main[18].

The Southampton to Salisbury canal

The use of water as a means of moving about and transporting goods had long been known to be much easier than travelling overland. Man had used the sea and larger rivers since prehistoric times, not only as a method of travelling around the British Isles, but also to transport heavy goods such as stone and timber. One horse can pull 50 – 100 tons along a good waterway, compared with up to 2 tons on a level road, and considerably less up steep uneven tracks. Much effort was put into making rivers navigable as far upstream as possible by removing obstructions and dredging. Weirs were used to deepen rivers, and locks to raise or lower the level of boats, and by 1724 there were 1,160 miles of river navigation in England, and most of England was within 15 miles of a navigable river. Goods were beginning to be moved around the country more freely and at less cost[19].

Canals had been cut in other countries, and had been constructed in England to a limited extent, but the concept of canal transport playing a major part in improving industrial development received a considerable boost when the Duke of Bridgewater, and his engineer James Brindley, built a canal to take coal directly from the mines at Worsley to the cotton mills a few miles away in Manchester. The canal was finally opened in 1761 and this engineering feat heralded the beginning of the canal-building era, which lasted until 1840. Hitherto industrial works had had to be built where the raw materials were found, and the products were sold locally.

Canals enabled trade to be extended to different parts of the country, and coal could be brought in as the energy source for industrial processes, as well as providing towns and villages with heating fuel[20]. However, there was often some local opposition to the idea of river or canal transport; watermill owners feared the loss of water from the millstream, farmers were concerned that their water meadow systems would be affected or their fields flooded, turnpike trustees realised that the use of a convenient canal would reduce their revenue from tolls, and wagon carriers were afraid that they would lose their livelihood.

Although many of the canals built following the success of the Bridgewater canal were designed to make movement between principal towns easier, another valuable function of the waterways was to connect seaports with inland areas. Imported goods and raw materials could then be transported inland more easily, and local produce could reach a seaport for shipping round the coast, or across the channel. Southampton was a port which needed better access to inland regions, since neither the Test nor the Itchen rivers were navigable. The city of Salisbury did not have a good link with the coast, as attempts to make the Avon navigable had not met with any measurable success. From contemporary maps and later archaeological surveys it appears that work was carried out on the Avon between 1675 and 1730 to construct various canal sections to bypass obstacles in the river, and for a short time this did make it navigable as far as Salisbury for 25 ton barges. In spite of this, there was never any sustained enthusiasm in Salisbury to make the Avon into an economically viable waterway, and the city traders continued to use the overland route to Southampton[21].

The Andover and the Southampton to Salisbury Canals were therefore conceived as the solution to improving the movement of goods in Hampshire and south Wiltshire. The Andover Canal was to be cut parallel to the river Test to take goods to and from Andover, Stockbridge and Romsey, and the Southampton and Salisbury Canal would use part of it south of Kimbridge, with a section leaving it at Redbridge and running through an 880 yard tunnel leading to Southampton docks at Northam. A second canal would branch off at Kimbridge and lead along the Dun Valley to Alderbury, where it would go through a tunnel into the Avon Valley to join a section running down from Salisbury along the valley beside the river Avon[22] (Fig. 34).

An Act of Parliament was necessary before a canal could be constructed, to give

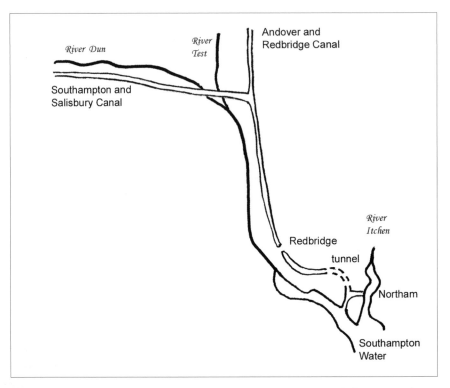

Fig. 34 *Part of the proposed route of the Southampton and Salisbury Canal.(MB)*

permission for such matters as the compulsory purchase of land, the diversion of streams and the crossing of highways. In 1795 an Act was passed for the construction of the Southampton and Salisbury Canal[23].

An Act for making and maintaining a navigable canal from the town and county of Southampton to the city of New Sarum in the county of Wilts, with a collateral branch to Northam.

The Company of Proprietors of the Southampton and Salisbury Canal was to be formed, which would be empowered to make a navigable cut. Detailed descriptions are given in the Act concerning how the canal was to be managed and run. Stones and posts to give distances were to be placed at one quarter of a mile apart. No pits for gravel, marl, stones, peat or chalk were to be dug within 20 yards of the canal without consent. It would be lawful for owners of land adjoining the navigation to use pleasure boats and boats to move animals around the farm etc in boats up to 7 feet in breadth, but not to pass through any lock without permission and not to block the towpath or obstruct boats using the canal, nor to leave boats moored on the canal.

In 1795 Joseph Hill of Romsey was appointed as engineer to the canal project, and Edward Gee of Lockerley contracted to excavate the canal from Kimbridge to West Grimstead. Not all the contractors were local men; the masons, who were to construct two aqueducts to carry the canal over the river Test to its junction with the Andover Canal, came from Wolverhampton, and a carpenter from Birmingham would make the lock gates. There was to be a 2 ½ mile summit section across the high ground near Alderbury, where water would be supplied by local streams, and a reservoir was to be constructed on each side of this saddle of land. The canal was to pass through a hundred yard-long tunnel at Alderbury, to avoid having to build a viaduct to carry the turnpike road over the canal. Gee's work included digging and banking the canal, and puddling it to make it watertight. He was also to make the reservoir near West Grimstead, capturing part of the source of the River Dun[24, 25].

Work began on the canal in 1796 and on December 8th 1802 the hatches of the reservoir at West Grimstead were opened, filling the feeder to the summit. The lock gates were opened, and water began to flow down to West Dean. This was very encouraging and a visible sign of progress on the canal, but there were major difficulties at both ends of it. The Southampton tunnel had not been cut through, and there was no canal connection between West Grimstead and Salisbury. The construction of the Dun Valley section had not been without its problems; the summer of 1798 had been so wet that brickmaking for the locks and bridges had to stop, and when the Dun finally burst its banks after a deluge in February 1799, it carried away the bridge at West Dean and swept down the valley, damaging the canal works as it did so. The disruption in the villages and the countryside during those years must have been considerable even without floods, and the bands of navigators, or navvies, appears to have given the local population some problems. During the 1790s a group of nuns, who had fled from Flanders during the French revolution, were allowed to live in West Dean House, which had been unoccupied for some time. The disruption caused by the canal construction, and the presence of the navvies, upset them to such an extent that they fled the area[26].

By 1803 the canal was navigable from Kimbridge as far as the 13th lock on the summit at Alderbury Common, from where a wooden tramway led to the Salisbury to Southampton turnpike road to Salisbury. The canal basin at West Dean had been formed in 1802 and the towpath there widened to form a wharf[27, 28]. The canal link between Southampton and Salisbury must have started to look like a viable enterprise to the local inhabitants, with boats now able to come up and down from Redbridge, bringing coal which had formerly been transported by cart, as appears in Augustine Stevens's accounts, and carrying away timber from the woodland. The Andover Canal had already been completed in 1796, and was transporting coal and building materials from Southampton Water to Romsey, Stockbridge and Andover[29].

The canal network, which was steadily expanding across Britain, was at its most useful in the movement of bulky materials of low unit value, such as coal, lime and corn, and at a time of rapid urban development, bricks and timber. Although there were some broad canals, most of them, like the Southampton and Salisbury Canal, were narrow canals which could take boats up to 70-72 feet long by 6 feet 10 inches wide, and carrying 25-30 tons. However, goods often still had to be unloaded into carts to reach their final destination[30]. By 1810 water routes linked the majority of sizeable towns in England. It was difficult to link up a national network, since most canals had been built in isolation to provide for local needs, which had led to a lack of standardisation in the waterways and the size of boats which could use them. Nevertheless, the canals revolutionised the transport system in Britain, and helped to stimulate agricultural and industrial change[31].

Unfortunately, the Southampton and Salisbury Canal proved to be a total disaster; the Salisbury section of the canal was never dug, and the Southampton end which left the Andover Canal at Redbridge was never completed. The Dun Valley section had cost £90,000 and it was estimated that it would cost a further £9950 to complete the work, and £2000 for repairs. The canal was considered unlikely to bring in sufficient money to cover the costs, and the whole project was abandoned in 1807[32].

Remnants of the canal can still be seen along the valley, although its course was disrupted by the building of the railway some 40 years later. Most of the locks have disappeared, although there are the remains of Lock 4 clearly visible at Holbury Lane, Lockerley. There is also a well-preserved original bridge in East Grimstead adjacent to the church, and other remains at various places along the valley (Figs.XXII, XXIII, p167).

The coming of the railway

In the latter part of the 18th and the early 19th centuries a number of unconnected engineering developments were taking place. The concept that hauling vehicles bearing heavy loads on smooth rails was much easier than along a rough road had been known, and utilised to a limited extent, since the Middle Ages, and some form of trackways were thought to have been used in Roman times. Early rails were wooden, and simple tramways using rectangular bars of wood were developed to carry coal in mines, collieries and quarries in the 17th century. During the 18th century metal plating of the rails was used to prolong the life of the wood, and from this, the idea of using metal rails, and shaping them to hold the wagon wheels gradually developed. Horses pulled the wagons, and the use of ' rail-ways' was extended to moving heavy materials over fairly short distances in a variety of circumstances.

Fig. 35 *Railway station scene. (J. Leech, in Punch,1860)*

Another development which happened around the same time was the use of steam power in stationary engines for such tasks as pumping water out of mine shafts, burning coal as the energy source. From this the application of steam to propel a vehicle along a road was developed, together with the many other uses which could be made of steam power[33]. During the 19th century steam engines began to make their appearance around the countryside, and traction engines were widely employed by the 1850s, by which time steam was replacing manpower and horsepower for tasks such as threshing and winnowing the corn. The natural progression was to have steam locomotives pulling wagons along on metal rails, and to aid the development of this new concept improved methods of manufacturing steel for railway lines and boiler plate became commercially viable at about the same time.

These developments were taking place during the heyday of the turnpike roads, and when the expansion of the canals seemed to be the best way of transporting bulky or heavy goods over long distances. All these different methods of transportation did not operate in isolation. Wooden rails were often used to haul materials to a canal for transport, and where the transported goods were needed some distance from a canal wharf, they were loaded onto carts for the last part of the journey by road. However, the development of the railway gathered momentum, and in 1830 the first public steam-powered passenger and freight line in southern England was opened in Kent, albeit only a single line six miles long. By the late 1830s three main lines from London were being constructed, to Dover, Brighton and Southampton, and by 1845 there were about 4,500 miles of railways in Great Britain. The turnpike trusts and canal companies put up some resistance, but the railways won the day and a whole new means of transport was created within about 20 years[34].

There was considerable competition between the railway companies to extend the rail network westwards. The London and South Western Railway opened their Eastleigh to Salisbury line, which ran along the Dun Valley, in 1847, the line terminating at a station in the Milford end of Salisbury. During the following ten years Salisbury gained connections in other directions. In 1856 the Wiltshire, Somerset and Weymouth Railway opened a line to Warminster, which was a broad-gauge track to connect up with the Great Western Railway lines, and they built their Salisbury station in Fisherton. A direct line from London to Salisbury opened in 1857 which terminated at Milford, and in 1859 a line from Salisbury (Fisherton) to Yeovil extended the railway further west. Connecting lines were built across Salisbury between Fisherton and Milford, or rather underneath as it involved a tunnel, and the Warminster line converted to standard gauge in 1874. After this conversion, and further extension of the line to connect with Bristol, trains could run through from the coal fields of South Wales via Salisbury and Eastleigh to Southampton. Passenger trains between Cardiff, Bristol and Portsmouth began in 1896 and from Eastleigh there were lines to London and Southampton[35, 36].

The construction of the Eastleigh to Salisbury railway line must have caused much the same disruption to life along the Dun Valley as the cutting of the canal less than 50 years before. Those inhabitants old enough to have witnessed both events must have wondered whether this new venture was any more likely to succeed than the previous one. In 1847, when the line was completed, there were stations at West Dean and Dunbridge, and at Romsey there was a connection with the Southampton to Andover line.

West Dean station lies on the county boundary, almost adjacent to the remains of the old canal wharf. The principal buildings were on the down (towards Salisbury) side of the track, and included a large, solid station master's house, now converted into two separate dwellings. On the other side, beyond the platform, there were goods yards, which included cattle pens and a 5 ton crane for loading[37].

Further down the line stood Dunbridge station, the characteristic shape of which can be seen in the distance in a drawing made in 1849, two years after the line was opened (Fig. XXIV, p170). In the late 19th century Dunbridge Mill, a steam roller mill, was built near the station. Mills powered by steam, using coal as the energy source, no longer needed to be situated where they could utilize water or wind power. A mill adjacent to the railway could have regular supplies of coal delivered directly from distant coal depots, and in addition there was an easy means of transport for the sacks of flour to the towns.

The development of the turnpike roads, followed by the construction of first the canal and then the railway, must have made an enormous difference to the outlook of the people who lived in the villages along the Dun Valley, particularly as the changes all happened within two or three generations. By the 1850s communication with the rest of the country was a daily affair, people could travel to Salisbury or Southampton whenever they needed to, and farm equipment, building materials and household items could be purchased from distant sources and collected from the local station. The Rev.G.S. Master, who lived in West Dean, commented in 1885[38]:

A branch of the London and South-Western Railway, opened in 1847, and having a station at West Dean, has, since that date, afforded ample facilities of communication, Romsey and Salisbury being accessible in a quarter-of-an-hour, Southampton in an hour, and London in less than three.

Fuel for heating and cooking no longer involved spending many hours cutting or gathering wood from the woodland or hedgerow, as coal arrived by train. The days of droving to take farm animals to far-off markets and fairs were over, the animals were now driven down to the railway yards and loaded into cattle wagons. Fresh milk could be delivered to the towns from the countryside on a regular basis, and letters and parcels could be sent in both directions. Ease of transport was not the only dramatic change in the 19th century which affected the rural way of life, but it certainly played an important part.

Appendix I

The Dun Valley probate inventories which were used to provide the information in Chapter 6.

1563	Richard Lodge, cleric, East Tytherley	
1573	Hugh Hatcher, husbandman, Lockerley	
1581	William Canterton, gent, Kimbridge	£41
1582	Robert Gynes, husbandman, Lockerley	£16
1583	Nicholas Blake, East Dean	£40
1586	Robert Moody, East Dean	
1589	Steven Fox, East Dean	£40
1591	John Prangnell, East Tytherley	£31
1592	John Symes, husbandman, East Dean	
1592	Absolom Blanchard, East Dean (HRO 21M65/D3/163)	
1592	William Ireland, East Dean	
1594	John Russon, sen, Lockerley	£62
1594	Eleanor Pragnell, East Tytherley	£33
1597	John Moore, husbandman, East Tytherley	£120
1600	Robert Wrathe, yeoman, Lockerley	£7 7 debts of £15
1604	Peter Ireland, East Tytherley	
1610	Agnes Pragnell, Lockerley	£24
1618	Edward Damerham, husbandman, West Dean	£68
1619	Edward Blackford, cleric, Lockerley	£70
1626	Tristram Howet, Lockerley (born 1619 Huet)	£17
1629	George Fox, yeoman, East Dean	£200
1631	George Webb, husbandman, East Tytherley	£74
1631	Margery Ireland, East Tytherley	£133
1631	George Webb, husbandman, East Tytherley	£74
1637	Robert Wheatley, cleric, East Dean	£43
1638	Thomas Dangerfield, yeoman, East Dean	£408
1638	Richard Bennet, Lockerley	£17
1638	Robert Tutt, gent, Lockerley	£228
1638	Richard Bonner, East Tytherley	£34
1640	John Kent, yeoman, East Dean	£90
1649	Augustine Betteridge, husbandman,Lockerley	£9
1653	Nicholas Smith, husbandman, East Tytherley	£21
1669	George Fox, weaver, East Dean	£35
1669	Christopher Dobbs, surgeon, East Tytherley	£42

1670	Richard Bonner, husbandman,East Tytherley	£32
1674	William Marsh, pipe maker, Lockerley	£12
1679	Silvester Langridge, blacksmith, East Tytherley	£91
1681	Richard Vaughan, yeoman, Lockerley	£15
1688	Edward Hinxman, blacksmith, West Dean	
1689	William Marsh, pipe maker, Lockerley	£18
1691	George Ventham, yeoman, East Tytherley	£178
1690	Thomas Hatcher, carpenter, Lockerley	£28
1692	William Neate, butcher, Lockerley	£83
1694	Thomas Gilbert, yeoman, Lockerley	£165
1730	John Hobbs, butcher, Lockerley	

Appendix II

Hants Hearth Tax, 1665. See Chapter 10, the population of the Dun Valley.

East Dean

Hearths chargeable

Henry Whithead esq	8	Mr Richard Ashley	5	William Row	3
Alexander Thomas	1	Widow Fox	3	Edward Huchman	1
Widow Grantham	1	Widow Thistlethwayt	2	Widow Lambe	1
George Fox, jun.	2	Robert Browne	1	George Langridge	1
Mark Bettridge	2	Thomas Gray	1	Edward Gray	1
James Spragg	4	Widow Snow	2	Edward Spragg	4
Richard Loaght	2	John Moseam	1	Robert Terry	1

Hearths not chargeable

Henry Pinnock	1	Robert Mondy	1	Robert Mondy	2
Widow Earland	1	Francis Rogers	1	Widow Carter	1
Thomas Oastler	1	Richard Canterton	1	Thomas Southwell	1
Robert Shaffling	1	John Roe	1	Robert Talmage	2
Roger Southwell	1				

Lockerley

Hearths chargeable

Dr Barlow	12	Mr Francklyn	4	Mr Thistlethwaite	7
Thomas Lane	5	Mistress Hurst & Mr Clifford	4		
Mabel Bennett, widow	1	Mr Gifford	4	John Martin	4
Richard Wingham	2	Edward Spragge	2	Thomas Collins	2
Thos & Richard Rose	2	William Yoinge	1	William Mersh	3
William Baldwyn	2	George Pragnell	2	Widow Skilton	1
Nicholas Matthew	1	John Cottshall	1	Edward Dangerfield	1
Mark Betteridge	1	Dr Dobbs	1	John Ventham	2
Richard Rose	1	Richard Hatcher	1	John Blake	1
Thomas Mersh	1	Thomas Hatcher	1	Nicholas Course	1
Mr Brace	6	Austin Russen	1	William Wheable	2
Widow Baldwin	1				

Hearths not chargeable

William Woodford	1	William Pearce	1	Thomas Pearce, sen.	1

Robert Pike	1	Thomas Pike	1	Tristram Mundy	1
...... Brooker	1	Richard Wingham	1	Nicholas Hancock	1
William Stock	1	Nicholas Gynes, sen	1	Nicholas Gynes, jun	1
Widow Woodford	1	John Arthur	1	John Andrews	1
Margaret Godden	1	Stephen Arthur	1	Richard Major	1
Widow Godden	1	John Bedford	1	Ann Bedford	1
Ralph Tubb	1	Alexander Newman	1	Andrew Blake	1
Joan Lynhm	1	John Perrier	1	John Pragnell	1
Widow Cleeter	1	Widow Martyne	1	Henry Mersh	1
Elizabeth Finch	1	Nicholas Wilkins	1		

East Tytherley

Hearths chargeable

Mr Francis Rowle	32	George Forest	1	Silvester Langradge	3
George Ventham	2	Alexander Whitcher	3	Richard Bonner	1
Widow Woodford	1	Alexander Linton	1	Thomas Downes	1
William Bedridge	1	George Earles	2	Edward Dangerfield	1
Edward Dangerfield, jun	4	Christopher Dobbs	2	William Williams	2
Cuthbert Wheatland	3	William Blackford	3	Richard Bonner, jun	1
George Forest	5	Robert Ventham	1	Silvester Langradge	1
Silvester Webb	1	Nicholas Kingman	1	Elizabeth Ventham	1

Hearths not chargeable

John Davis	1	Widow Stent	1	John Stent	1
Walter Gootley	1	Widow Morrock	1	John Bonnily	1
John Littlefield	1	Nicholas Ventham	1	Nicholas Briant	1
Robert Cole	1	Henry Case	1	Widow Austin	1
Garrett Earles	1	John Fabine	1		

Hearth Tax was charged on the occupier, not the landlord. A person was exempt if he did not pay poor or church rate, his house was worth less than 20s per year, or his land, goods and chattels were worth less than £10 per year. It was not payable on furnaces, kilns, hospitals, almshouses where the revenue or endowment did not exceed £100 per year.

1664 The owner had to pay if he let buildings out separately from the house to which they had formerly belonged, or sub-divided a house.

References

Abbreviations

HRO	Hampshire Record Office, Winchester.
WSHC	Wiltshire and Swindon History Centre, Chippenham.
WANHM	Wilts. Archaeol. and Natural History Magazine.
VCHW	Victoria County History of Wiltshire.
VCHH	Victoria County History of Hampshire.
TNA	The National Archives, Kew.
Cal. Close.	Calendar of Close Rolls
Cal. Pat.	Calendar of Patent rolls
Cal. Chart.	Calendar of Charter Rolls
Inq, PM.	Inquisition Post Mortem

Chap. 1 Setting the Scene

1. Barron, R.S. (1976) *The Geology of Wiltshire*. Moonraker Press, Bradford-on-Avon. pp 114-5, 144-150.
2. Toghill, P. (2000) *The Geology of Britain*. Swan Hill Press, Shrewsbury. pp 162-3.
3. Gelling, M. (2000) *Place-Names in the Landscape*. Phoenix Press, London. p 140, 97.
4. Cunliffe, B. (2003) *Wessex to AD 1000*. Pearson Education Ltd, Harlow. pp 275-80.
5. Ibid. p 302.
6. Ibid. pp 316-320.
7. Ibid. p 121.

Chap. 2 Medieval Times

1. Edwards, P. (1991) *Farming Sources for Local Historians*. Batsford Ltd. London. pp 116-127.
2. Stuart, D. (1992) *Manorial Records*. Phillimore, Chichester. pp 1-2.
3. Thorn, C. & Thorn, F. (1979) *Domesday Book* 6 *Wilts*. Gen. Ed. Morris, J. Phillimore, Chichester.
4. VCHH 4 East Tytherley parish. pp 498-500.
5. Prestwich, M. (2005) *Plantagenet England 1225-1360*. Clarendon Press, Oxford. pp 165-175.
6. VCHW 4 Royal forests. Grant, R. pp 391-434.
7. Baskerville, M. (2008) The boundaries of Buckholt, a Hampshire Royal Forest. *Hampshire Studies*. 63 pp 179-192.

8. Winchester, A (2000) *Discovering Parish Boundaries*. Shire Books. pp 11-20.

9. VCHW 1 pt. 1, Archaeological Gazetteer, enclosures and hillforts. Grinsell, L.V. pp 261-271.

10. Creighton, O.H. (2000) Early castles in the medieval landscape of Wiltshire. WANHM **93** pp 105-19.

11. Higham, R & Barker, P. (1992) *Timber Castles*. Batsford, London. pp 26-38.

12. Colt Hoare, R. (1837) The parish of West Dean. *The History of Modern Wiltshire* **5** *Alderbury*. pp 17-205.

13. Master, G.S. (1885) Collections for a history of West Dean. WANHM **22** pp 239-316.

14. VCHW (1959) Crittall, E. (Ed) **4** Royal forests. Grant, R. pp 391-434.

15. Inquisition of Oliver de Ingham 1344 *Abstracts of the Inq. Post Mortems relating to Wilts. from the reign of Edward III pt.3* Wilts. Archeol. & Nat. Hist. Soc. p 159.

16. Partition of the lands of Oliver de Ingham 1348 *Ibid.* p 193.

17. Baskerville, M. & Lambert, D. (2005) *A History of Bentley Wood*. The Friends of Bentley Wood, Salisbury. p 84.

18. Landsberg, S. (undated) *The Medieval Garden*. British Museum Press. pp 13-16.

19. Wood, M (1965) *The English Medieval House*. Bracken Books, London. pp 155-163.

20. Cantor, L. (1987) *The Changing English Countryside 1400-1700*. Routledge and Kegan Paul, London. pp 14-15.

21. Inquisition of Mary, wife of Steven Tumby, 1349. *Abstracts of the Inq. Post mortems relating to Wilts. from the reign of Edward III.* Wilts. Archeol. & Nat. Hist. Soc.p 209.

22. Master, G.S. As above.

23. Baskerville, M. & Lambert, D. As above. pp 30-32.

24. VCHH 1 Domesday Survey. Round, H. pp 399- 526.

25. VCHH **4** East Tytherley parish. pp 515-518.

26. Bond, J. (1994) Forests, chases, warrens and parks. *The medieval landscape of Wessex*. Ed. by Aston, M. and Lewis, C. Oxbow Books, Oxford. pp 115-159.

27. *Cal. Chart.* 1270. 1257-1300 p 151 (1906).

28. Rowley, T (1986) *The High Middle Ages 1200-1550*. Paladin Grafton Books, London. 64.

29. *Cal. Pat.* 1374. 1370-74 p 400. (1914).

30. *Cal. Pat.* 1357. 1354-58 p 526. (1909).

31. *Cal. Pat.* 1391. 1388-92 p 501. (1902).

32. *Cal. Pat.* 1392. 1391-96 p 58. (1905).

33. *Cal. Pat.* 1496. 1494-1509 p 85. (1916).

34. VCHH **4** Lockerley parish. pp 500-02.

35. *Cal. Chart.* 1271. 1257-1300 p 177. (1906).

36. VCHH **4** Lockerley parish. pp 500-502.

37. VCHH **4** East Dean parish. pp 498-500.

38. *Cal. Pat.* 1291. 1281-92 p 424. (1893)

39. *Cal. Pat.* 1355. 1354-58 p 198. (1909).

40. Inq. P.M. of John Whitehede esq. 1486. *Inq. P. M. Henry VII* 1 p 84. no.185 (1898).

41. VCHH **4** East Dean parish. pp 498-500.

42. VCHH **4** Mottisfont parish. pp 503-510.

Chap. 3   The Landscape

1. WSHC 776/399 Map of East Dean parish circa 1830.

2. WSCH 492/41/2 An agreement to enclose East Grimstead Common, 1723.

3. Richardson, A (2005) *The Forest, Park and Palace of Clarendon, c. 1200 - c. 1650.* BAR British Series 387. p 35.

4. Sheail, J. (1971) *Rabbits and their History.* Country Book Club, Newton Abbot. pp 49-51.

5. Baskerville, M. & Lambert, D. (2005) *A History of Bentley Wood.* The Friends of Bentley Wood, Salisbury. pp 46-52

6. Rackham, O. (2003) *Ancient Woodland.* Castlepoint Press, Dalbeattie. p 145.

7. Baskerville, M (2009) The use of the land in Buckholt, a Hampshire royal forest, 1200-1900. *Hampshire Studies.* **64** pp 200-222.

8. Baskerville, M. & Lambert, D. As above. pp 84-5.

9. Watts, M. (2005) *Water and Wind Power.* Shire Publications. pp 5-25.

10. *Curia Regis Rolls* **2** 1201-3 p 108.

11. *Feet of Fines for Wilts. for the reign of Edward III.* 1352. Wilts. Archeol. & Nat. Hist. Soc. p 100 no. 407 (1974).

12. *Calendar of Memoranda Rolls (Exchequer)* 1326. 1326-7 p 332 (1968).

13. HRO 5M58/513 Lease of Holbury Mill with land in East Dean, Lockerley and East Tytherley, 1689.

14. HRO 3M49/31 Conveyance of the manors of East Tytherley and Lockerley, 1654

15. *Cal. Close.* 1256. 1254-56 p 332 (1931).

16. Master, G. S. (1885) Collections for a history of West Dean. *WANHM* **22** pp 239-316.

Chap. 4   The Lords of the Manor

1. Master, G.S. (1885) Collections for a history of West Dean *WANHM* **22** pp 239-316.

2. Colt Hoare, R. (1837) The parish of West Dean. *The History of Modern Wiltshire* 5 *Alderbury*. pp 17-205.

3. Master, G.S. As above.

4. Fenton, C. (1961) The Evelyn family in Wiltshire. *WANHM* 58 pp 18-24.

5. Master, G.S. As above.

6. Grundy, I. (1999) *Lady Mary Wortley Montague*. Oxford University Press.

7. VCHH 4 East Dean parish. pp 498-500.

8. VCHH 4 West Tytherley parish. pp 519-524, 3 Millbrook parish. pp 427-432.

9. HRO 129M71/210 Legg, R.R. The history of East Tytherley school, 1994.

10. VCHH 4 East Tytherley parish. pp 515-518.

11. Beggs, B. & Beggs, D. (2005) *The Churches of the Test Valley*. Test Valley Churches Book Soc.

Chap. 5   Religion

1. Strong, R. (2007) *A Little History of the English Country Church*. Jonathan Cape, London. pp 23-4.

2. Master, G. S. (1885) *Collections for a history of West Dean*. WANHM. 22 pp 239-316.

3. Cox, J.C. & Ford,C. B. (1961) *Parish Churches*. Batsford, London. p 36.

4. Master, G.S. As above.

5. Cox, J.C. & Ford, C.B. As above p 21.

6. Kain, R. J. P. & Prince, H. C. (2000) *Tithe Surveys for Historians*. Phillimore, Chichester. pp 3-4.

7. HRO 35M48/16/117 East Tytherley Glebe Terrier, 1639.

8. HRO 21M65E15/88 Glebe terriers of Mottisfont, Lockerley and East Dean, 1690-1760.

9. Master, G.S. As above.

10. HRO 1637B/49 Probate inventory of Robert Wheatley, 1637.

11. Master, G.S. As above.

12. Strong, R. As above. pp 39-40.

13. Cook, G. H. (1948) *Medieval Chantries and Chantry Chapels*. Phoenix, London. pp 6-17.

14. Master, G.S. As above.

15. Knowles, D. & Hadcock, R. N. (1971) *Medieval Religious Houses in England and Wales*. Longman, London. p 17.

16. *Cal. Pat.* 1334. 1334-38. (1895).

17. Rushton, N. S. & Currie, C. K. (2001) Land management and custumal diversity of the estate of Mottisfont Priory in the 1340s. *Hants. Studies*. 56 pp 202-218.

18. Blake, E. O. (Ed.) (1981) *The Cartulary of the Priory of St. Denys Near Southampton.* **2** Southampton Univ. Press. p 240.

19. Ibid. p 238.

20. Ibid. p 187.

21. Ibid. p 188.

22. Ibid. p 182.

23. Ibid. p xlvi.

24. Trevelyan, G.M. (1946) *English Social History.* Longmans, London. p 110.

25. Ashley, M. (1990) *The English Civil War.* Sutton Publishing, Stroud. pp 12-13.

26. Strong, R. As above. pp 96-7.

27. Maclachlan, T. (2000) *The Civil War in Hampshire.* Rowanvale Press, Salisbury. pp 24-34.

28. Maclachlan, T. (1997) *The Civil War in Wiltshire.* Rowanvale Press, Salisbury. pp 200-205.

29. Wroughton, J. (1999) *An unhappy Civil War.* Landsdown Press. pp 278-9.

30. Ward, W. R. (1995) *Parson and Parish in 18th Century Hampshire: Replies to Bishops' Visitations.* Hants. Record Series **13** p 48, 179, 200.

31. Master, G.S. As above.

32. Vickers, J.A. (ed.) (1993) *The Religious Census of Hampshire 1851.* Hants. Record Series **12** p 114.

33. Ibid. p 112.

34. Hardy, D. (1979) *Alternative Communities in 19th Century England.* Longman, London. pp 53 – 58.

35. HRO 27A04/5 Folder of copies of notes on Harmony Hall and Queenwood College.

Chap. 6   Probate Inventories

1. Cox, N. & Cox, J. (1984-50) Probate inventories: the legal background. *The Local Historian* **16** pp 133-143.

2. HRO probate inventories.

3. Brown, R. J. (1979) *The English Country Cottage.* Hale, London. pp 85-88.

4. Hagen, A (1995) *A Second Handbook of Anglo-Saxon Food and drink.* Anglo-Saxon Books, Norfolk. pp 207-212.

5. HRO 9N60/6 The accounts of Augustine Stevens, bailiff of East Tytherley, 1680.

6. Trow-Smith, R. (1957) *A History of British Livestock Husbandry to 1700.* Routledge and Kegan Paul, London. pp 119-123.

7. Bettey, J. H. (1976) The probate inventories of Dorset farmers 1573-1670. *The Local Historian* **12** pp 228-234.

8. Evans, G. E. (1956) *Ask the Fellows Who Cut the Hay*. Faber and Faber, London. pp 70-71.

9. HRO Sir Henry Whithed's letter book 1 1601-14.

10. HRO 44M69G/32/19 The muster book of Richard Whithead esq. *c* 1632.

11. HRO 9M60/6 As above.

Chap. 7 Manor Court Rolls

1. HRO 5M58/ 1-38 Manor court rolls of the manor of East Tytherley and Lockerley.

2. Stuart, D. (1992) *Manorial Records*. Phillimore, Chichester. p 2.

3. HRO 5M58/628 The manor of Lockerley belonging to Denys Rolle, 1759.

4. WSHC CC/Chapter 198/1 A survey of the manor of East Dean and Lockerley, the property of the Dean and Chapter of Salisbury cathedral, 1797.

5. Urquart, J. (1983) *Animals on the Farm*. Macdonald and Co. London. p 30.

6. WSHC 1300/104 Letters from Alexander Tutt to Richard Wheeler, 1598.

7. Holt, R. (1988) *The Mills of Medieval England*. Blackwell, Oxford. pp 36-53.

8. Douglas, D. (Ed.) (1967) *English Historical Documents 1485-1588*. 5 Eyre and Spottiswood, London. pp 917-924.

9. Campbell, M. (1942) *The English Yeoman*. Merlin Press, UK. pp 158.

10. WSHC CC/Chapter 198/1 As above.

Chap. 8 The Accounts of Augustine Stevens

1. HRO 9M60/6 The accounts of Augustine Stevens, bailiff of east Tytherley, 1680.

2. Morrill, J. (Ed.) (1996) *The Oxford Illustrated History of Tudor and Stuart Britain*. Oxford University Press. p 4.

3. Davis, T. (1794) A general view of agriculture in the county of Wilts. *Review and Abstract of the County Reports to the Board of Agriculture*. William Marshall (1817). David and Charles Reprints, Newton Abbot (*c* 1968). pp 188-232.

4. VCHW 4 Agriculture *c* 1500-1793, Kerridge, E. pp 43-64.

5. Davis, T. (1794) A general view of the agriculture of the county of Wilts. *Review and Abstract of the County Reports to the Board of Agriculture*. William Marshall (1817). David and Charles Reprints, Newton Abbot (*c* 1968). pp 184-232.

6. Vancouver, C. (1813) A general view of the agriculture in Hants. Ibid. pp 301-352.

7. HRO 5M58/431-443 Indenture between Francis Rolle of Shapwicke and Joseph Hill of East Tytherley, Yeoman, 1708.

Chap. 9   Changes in the Countryside

1.   Bettey, J. (2005) *Wiltshire Farming in the 17th Century*. Wilts. Record Soc. 57 Chippenham. pp 136-157.

2.   Chapman, J. & Seeliger, S (1997) *Formal and Informal Enclosures in Hampshire 1700-1900*. Hants. Papers **12** Hants. Co. Council.

3.   WSHC 1369/8/16 Indenture of 1682 between Sir John Evelyn, Henry Whitehead and William Hussey.

4.   HRO 13M63/169 Lease of a messuage called Brocknes, in East Dean, 1692.

5.   HRO 11M56/55 Lease of a messuage in East Dean, 1716.

6.   HRO 5M58/628 The manor of Lockerley belonging to Denys Rolle, 1759.

7.   WRO CC/Chapter/198/1 A survey of the manor of East Dean and Lockerley, the property of the Dean and Chapter of Salisbury cathedral, 1797.

8.   HRO 5M58/485 Surrender of the tenants of the manor of East Tytherley of their interest in Thornes Wood or Common, 1755.

9.   Chapman, J. & Seeliger, S. As above.

10.   HRO 5M58/129 Extract from the award made by G. Barnes under the Act for Enclosure of Butler's Wood, *c* 1816.

11.   Hammond, J.L. & Hammond, B. (1913, reprinted 1987) *The Village Labourer 1760-1832*. Alan Sutton, Gloucester. pp 175-8.

12.   Holland, M. (ed) (2005) *Swing Unmasked*. Family and Community Historical Research Soc. pp 1-6.

13.   Chambers, J. (1996) *Hampshire Machine Breakers*. J. Chambers, Letchworth. p 57.

14.   Hobsbawn, E.J. & Rude, G. (1969) *Captain Swing*. Lawrence & Wishart, London. pp 116-129.

15.   Chambers, J. (1993) *Wiltshire Machine Breakers, 1 The Riots and Trials*. J. Chambers, Letchworth. pp 36-7.

16.   Ibid.

17.   Chambers, J. (1996) *Hampshire Machine Breakers*. As above pp 51, 121-8.

18.   HRO TOP 334/3/3 Extract of a letter dated East Tytherley, Nov. 22nd 1830.

19.   Hobsbawn, E. J. and Rude, G. As above. p 262.

20.   Stamp, L.D. (1955) *Man and the Land*. Collins, London. pp 103-4.

21.   Bettey, J. (2005) *Wiltshire Farming in the 17th Century*. Wilts. Record Soc. 57 Chippenham. p xxx.

22.   Cowan, M. (2005) *Wiltshire Water Meadows*. Hobnob Press, Salisbury.

23.   WSHC 1369/8/16 The several answer of Sir John Evelyn to ye Bill of Complaint of Henry Whithed, 1682.

24.   Ellis, W. (*c* 1772) *Ellis's Husbandry*. 1 pp 49-54.

25.   HRO 25M94/3 A survey of land in East Tytherley, Lockerley and East Dean, 1829.

26.   HRO 25M94/3 as above.

Chap. 10   The Shaping of the Post-Medieval Community

1. Cook, C. & Wroughton, J. (1980) *English Historical Facts 1603-1688.* MacMillan, London. pp 90-6.

2. Nash, A. (1988) The population of southern England in 1086: a new look at the evidence of Domesday Book. *Southern History* 10 pp 1-28.

3. Thorn, C. & Thorn, F. (eds.) (1979) *Domesday Book 6 Wiltshire* Section 37. Phillimore, Chichester.

4. VCHH 1 The holders of lands. pp 449-526.

5. Ramsay, G.D. (ed.) (1954) Two 16th century taxation lists, 1545 and 1576. WANHM 10 pp viii-ix

6. Ibid. p 128.

7. Vick, D.F. (ed.) (1987) *West Hampshire Lay subsidy Assessments 1558-1603.* HRO H336. 23094227. pp 8-11.

8. Hughes, E. & White, P. (eds.) *Hampshire Hearth Tax Assessment 1665.* Hants. Record Series 11 pp 256-266.

9. HRO parish registers.

10. Master, G.S. (1885) Collections for a history of West Dean. WANHM 22 pp 239-316.

11. VCHH 5 Table of population, Minchin, G.S. pp 435-450.

12. The Census Returns of England and Wales, 1831. 2 pp 564-5, 690.

13. Winchester Quarter Sessions. (HRO)

14. Winchester Quarter Sessions Calendar of prisoners, Winchester House of Correction, 1750.

15. Winchester Lent Assizes 1828. (HRO)

16. Williams, C.H. (1967) An act against vagabonds and beggars, 1495. *English Historical Documents 1485-1558.* 5 pp 1023-4.

17. Ibid. An act concerning punishment of beggars and vagabonds, 1531. p 1025- 7.

18. Tate, W.E. (1983) *The English Parish Chest.* Phillimore, Chichester. pp 192-3.

19. HRO 19M82/PO1/37 Settlement certificate for Michael Ireland, 1746.

20. HRO Q9/2/5/2 Removal order for Martha Edwards and her children, 1751.

21. Williams, C.H. (1967) An act for punishment of sturdy vagabonds and beggars 1536. *English Historical Documents 1485-1558.* pp 1028-9.

22. HRO 44M69/G3/203 Petition on behalf of Richard Bonner, 1630.

23. HRO 47M/66/1 Overseer's accounts for Lockerley, 1771- 94.

24. Ibid.

25. HRO 47M/66/4 Letter to Mrs. Hillier, 1830.

26. Morrison, K. (1999) *The Workhouse. English Heritage.*

27. Reports of the commissions concerning charities and education, Wiltshire. (1839) 36 pp 449-50.

28. Ibid.

29. HRO 129M71/136 A parcel of land for East Tytherley school, 1717.

30. VCHH **2** The history of schools, Leach, A.F. pp 250-408.

31. Ward, W.R. (ed.) (1995) *Parson and Parish in 18th century Hants: replies to the Bishops' Visitations*. Hants. Record Series **13** p 48.

32. HRO 129M71/64 Trust deed establishing trustees for East Tytherley school under Sarah Rolle's 1718 trust, 1736.

33. HRO 129M71/210 Legg, R.R. (1999) East Tytherley School and the Sarah Rolle Foundation.

34. Handcock, W.D. (ed.) *English Historical Documents 1874-1914*. **12**(2). Eyre & Spottiswood. pp 483-4.

35. HRO 127M83/PJ1 Lockerley school manager's minutes, 1870-83.

36. HRO 128M83PJ2 East Dean school minutes.

37. Leyser, H. (1996) Women at work. *Medieval Women*. Phoenix, London. pp 142-67.

Chap. 11   Travel and transport

1. Wright, G.N. (1988) *Roads and Trackways of Wessex*. Moorland Publishing, Ashbourne. pp 33-36.

2. Baskerville, M. & Lambert, D. (2005) *A History of Bentley Wood*. The Friends of Bentley Wood, Salisbury. pp 18-21.

3. Cochrane, C. (1969) *The Lost Roads of Wessex*. Pan Books, London. pp 34-36.

4. Gerhold, D. (2005) *Carriers and Coachmasters*. Phillimore, Chichester. pp 112-3.

5. Chandler, J (1998) (ed) *Printed Maps of Wiltshire 1787-1844*. Wilts. Record Soc. **52** pp intro.

6.   Cochrane, C. as above. pp 122-129.

7. Addison, W. (1980) *The Old Roads of England*. Batsford, London. pp 84-87.

8. HRO Q23/2/78 Lockerley: Butler's Wood, 1815.

9. HRO PER42/72 Watts, G. Types of drove roads. *Hants. Field Club Newsletter*. 2004.

10. VCHW **4** Roads, Cossons, A. pp 254-271.

11. Wright, G.N. as above. pp 143-50.

12. HRO 61M85/3 An Act for more effectually repairing the roads leading from Romsey to Stockbridge and Wallop, 1826-7.

13. TNA F17/398 Plan of certain lands called Buckholt Wood, 1778.

14. Indenture of the sale of Norman Court, 1806. Author's copy.

15. HRO 5M58/262-87. Title deeds of a farm purchased by F.G. Dalgety from the trustees of H. Cooper, 1874.

16. Chambers, J. (1996) Hampshire Machine Breakers. J. Chambers, Letchworth, pp 121-8.

17. Albert, W. (1983) The turnpike trusts. Transport in the Industrial Revolution. ed. Aldcroft, D & Freeman, M. Manchester University Press. p 35.

18. VCHW 5 County government since 1835. Lewis, R.A. pp 231-295.

19. Hadfield, C. (1969) *British Canals*. David & Charles, Newton Abbot. p 18.

20. Hadfield, C. As above. pp 29-34.

21. Chandler, J.H. (1983) *Endless Street*. Hobnob Press, Salisbury. pp 128-30.

22. Vine, P.A.L. (1990) *Hampshire Waterways*. Middleton Press, Midhurst.

23. HRO 15M84Z1/34 An Act for making a navigable canal from Southampton to Salisbury, 1795.

24. Braun, H. (1962) The Salisbury canal – a Georgian misadventure. WANHM 58 pp 171-180.

25. Welch, E. (1966) *The Bankrupt Canal, Southampton and Salisbury 1795-1808*. Southampton Papers 5 City of Southampton.

26. Fenton, C. (1961) The Evelyn Family in Wiltshire. WANHM 58 pp 18-24.

27. Vine, P.A.L. As above.

28. Braun, H. As above.

29. Hadfield, C. (1955) *The Canals of Southern England*. Phoenix House, London. p 84.

30. Hadfield, C. (1969) *British Canals*. As above p 56.

31. Squires, R.W. (1979) *Canals Revived*. Moonraker Press, Bradford on Avon. p 11.

32. Vine, P.A.L. As above.

33. Nock, O.S. (1955) The Railway Engineers. Batsford, London. pp 16-30.

34. White, H.P. (1992) *A Regional History of the Railways of Great Britain 2 Southern England*. D. Thomas, Nairn, Scotland. pp 13-23.

35. Ibid. pp 155-7.

36. Chandler, J.H. (1983) *Endless Street*. Hobnob Press, Salisbury. pp 139-43.

37. Oakley, M. (2004) *Wiltshire Railway Stations*. Dovecote Press, Wimborne. pp 50-1.

38. Master, G.S. (1885) Collections for a history of West Dean. WANHM 22 pp 239-316.

General Index

Bold type numbers indicate pictures and
maps

Accounts, farm chap.8
- household 123-125
see parish overseers' accounts
Agriculture 12,33-35
- livestock production 138-139
- equipment 94
Aldermoor 111,113
Allotment 33,130
Amesbury *see manor, priory*
Assize 109
Avon, River 2,183

Bailey 18,20
Baptists 78,79
Bees 94
Bell's Corner **129**, 130
Bentley Farm 30,**105**
Bentley Wood 1,17,25,26,30,36,65,173
Black Death 23,24
Bishop's Visitations 72-74
Borbach chapel *see chantry chapels*
Brewing 89-90
Bridges 112
Brocknes 127
Broughton 3,4,32,165
Buckholt *see royal forests*
Butter making 90,93
Butler's Wood 30,105,**129**,**130**
Butts Green 30,107,127

Canals 182-186
- Andover Canal 183
- Salisbury-Southampton Canal **167**,184-186
Capital offences 151
Carter's Clay 104,105,130
Carter's Lake 104,105,113
Castle Hill 18,22
Catholicism 57,69,72
Cattle 92,116,117
Cavaliers *see Royalists*
Cebell's Cross 105
Census returns 148-149
Chalk 3,136,137-138
Chapels **78**,79
- Chantry 49,50,63-64

Cheese making 90
Christianity 6
Churches (parish) 58-64
- East Dean, St. Winfrid's **47**,59,76
- West Dean, St. Mary's 58-59,60,62,74,76
- West Dean, All Saints 62-63
- East Grimstead, Holy Trinity 59,76
- East Tytherley, St. Peter's **8**,45,60,76
- Lockerley, St. John's 59-60,**75**,76
Church, building 58-60,74-76,79
- fittings 72
- repairs 63
Churchwardens 144
Civil War 69-72
Clarendon *see royal forests*
Clothing 90-91
Coaches 174,**179**
Common, land 12,34,104-105
- rights 12,107-108,127
Conifers 140-141
Constable(parish) 144
Coppicing 16,36,**43**,121
Copyhold 103
Court Baron 13,103
Court Leet 13,103
Critchell's Green 30,107,127
Croft 22
Crops 95,96,118,120

Dean Hill 1,2,3,173
Dean Heath 107
Debts 99
Deer 16,27-28
Deer parks 27-28
Demesne land 11
Dissenters 72,73-74, *see also nonconformity*
Droves 177-178
Dun, River 1,2,3-**41**,**46**
Dunbridge 3, *see manor, railway station, mill*
Domesday survey 10,14,26,39,145
Drainage 139

East Dean 3,4, *see church, manor, mill, school*
East Grimstead 3,4, *see canal, church, manor*
East Tytherley 1,3,4 *see church, manor, mill, school*
Education 163-169

Persons Index

Appendices I and II and lists of minor names are not included